EZRA & NEHEMIAH

Israel Returns from Exile

John MacArthur

THOMAS NELSON

Since 1798

MacArthur Bible Studies

Ezra & Nehemiah: Israel Returns from Exile

© 2016 by John MacArthur

Published in Nashville, Tennessee, by Nelson Books, an imprint of Thomas Nelson. Nelson Books and Thomas Nelson are registered trademarks of HarperCollins Christian Publishing, Inc.

Originally published in association with the literary agency of Wolgemuth & Associates, Inc. Original layout, design, and writing assistance by Gregory C. Benoit Publishing, Old Mystic, CT.

"Unleashing God's Truth, One Verse at a Time®" is a trademark of Grace to You. All rights reserved.

Thomas Nelson titles may be purchased in bulk for educational, business, fund-raising, or sales promotional use. For information, please e-mail SpecialMarkets@ThomasNelson.com.

Scripture quotations are taken from the *New King James Version*. Copyright © 1982 by Thomas Nelson, Inc. Used by permission. All rights reserved.

Some material in the Introduction, "Keys to the Text," and "Exploring the Meaning" sections are taken from *The MacArthur Bible Commentary*, John MacArthur, copyright © 2005 Thomas Nelson Publishers.

ISBN 978-0-7180-3479-5

First Printing April 2016 / Printed in the United States of America

HB 11.28.2023

CONTENTS

INTRODUCTION

The Lord God had warned the nation of Israel that He would send them into foreign captivity if they persisted in idolatry. Yet the people had ignored Him—and the prophets He sent to warn them—and had run headlong into disobedience. True to His word, God used the Assyrians and the Babylonians to evict Israel from its land, destroy the city of Jerusalem, and plunder the temple. With the people in captivity, it appeared Israel had no hope and no future.

However, God had also promised the captivity of Israel would last for only seventy years. At the end of that time, He raised up men such as Zerubbabel, Ezra, and Nehemiah to lead His people back to Jerusalem and begin rebuilding the city. He then sent several prophets, including Haggai and Zechariah, to encourage His people to continue the rebuilding efforts. Under this godly leadership, the people of Israel got a new start. Unfortunately—and predictably—they failed again and went back to their former idolatrous ways.

In these twelve studies, we will examine the events that led to the people being allowed to return to their homeland and what took place during the first two waves of their return. We will see how God raised up leaders among the exiles to not only champion the rebuilding efforts but also to protect the people from outside attack and turn them back to the worship of the Lord. We will discover what it means to put God first and see that apart from the new covenant and the Messiah, none of us would be able to be righteous before the Lord.

Through it all, we will learn some precious truths about the character of God, and we will see His great faithfulness in keeping His promises. We will learn, in short, what it means to follow Him wholeheartedly, walk by faith, and remain committed to His Word.

THE BOOK OF EZRA

Even though Ezra's name does not enter the account of Judah's post-exilic return to Jerusalem until 7:1, the book bears his name (which means "Jehovah helps") as a title. This is because both Jewish and Christian traditions attribute authorship to this famous scribe-priest. New Testament writers do not quote from the book of Ezra.

AUTHOR AND DATE

Ezra was most likely the author of both Ezra and Nehemiah, which might have originally been one book. After his arrival in Jerusalem in 458 BC, he changed from writing in the third person (Ezra 1–6) to writing in the first person (Ezra 7–10). In the earlier section, it is likely that he used the third person because he was quoting from his memoirs.

As a scribe, Ezra had access to the myriad of administrative documents that are found in the books of Ezra and Nehemiah. Few people were allowed access to the royal archives of the Persian Empire, but Ezra proved to be the exception. He was a strong and godly man who lived at the time of Nehemiah, and tradition says he was founder of the Great Synagogue, where the complete Old Testament canon was first formally recognized.

BACKGROUND AND SETTING

In 605–586 BC, God chastened His people because of their continued unfaithfulness to His covenant and allowed the Babylonians to sack and nearly depopulate Jerusalem. However, God promised that after seventy years of captivity the people would be allowed to return. The fulfillment of this prophecy began in 539 BC when Cyrus the Great, king of Persia, overthrew the Babylonians. Ezra begins a decree from Cyrus one year later that allowed the Jews to return to Jerusalem. The book chronicles the reestablishment of Judah's national calendar of feasts and sacrifices, including the rebuilding of the second temple.

Just as there had been three waves of deportation from Israel into Babylon (605 BC, 597 BC, and 586 BC), so there would be three returns to Jerusalem during a nine-decade span. Zerubbabel led the first return in 538 BC. Ezra led the second return in 458 BC. Nehemiah led the third return thirteen years later in 445 BC. However, the Jewish people's uncontested political autonomy never returned. The prophets Haggai and Zechariah preached during Zerubbabel's time, beginning about 520 BC.

HISTORICAL AND THEOLOGICAL THEMES

The Jews' return from the Babylonian captivity seemed like a second Exodus, sovereignly patterned in some ways after Israel's first redemption from Egyptian bondage. The return trip from Babylon involved activities similar to those of the original Exodus: (1) the rebuilding of the temple and the city walls; (2) the reinstitution of the law, which made Zerubbabel, Ezra, and Nehemiah collectively seem like a second Moses; (3) the challenge of the local enemies; and (4) the people's temptation to intermarry with non-Jews, resulting in idolatry.

The primary message of Ezra is that God orchestrated the past grim situation (captivity) and would continue to work through a pagan king and his successors to give Judah hope for the future (return). Ezra's message was that God's administration overrode that of any kings of this world, and He would continue to extend His covenant grace toward Israel. Another prominent theme is opposition from the local Samaritan residents, whose ancestors had been imported from Assyria. After being shunned from participating in the rebuilding of the temple, these enemies hired counselors to conspire against the Jews, but the Lord (through the preaching of Haggai and Zechariah) rekindled the spirit of the people and their leaders.

INTERPRETIVE CHALLENGES

There are a number of interpretive challenges in the book of Ezra. First, how do the post-exilic historical books of 1 and 2 Chronicles, Ezra, Nehemiah, and Esther relate to the post-exilic prophetic books of Haggai, Zechariah, and Malachi? The two books of Chronicles serve as a reminder of the promised Davidic kingship, the Aaronic priesthood, and appropriate temple worship. Haggai and

Zechariah prophesied during the period of Ezra 4–6, when temple construction was resumed. Malachi wrote during Nehemiah's revisit to Persia.

Second, what purpose does the book serve? Historically, Ezra reported the first two of three post-exilic returns to Jerusalem from the Babylonian captivity (Zerubbabel's in 538 BC and Ezra's in 458 BC). Spiritually, Ezra reestablished the importance of the Aaronic priesthood, encouraged the rebuilding of the second temple, and dealt with the people's gross sin of intermarriage with foreigners. Most importantly, he described how the sovereign hand of God moved kings and overcame opposition to reestablish Israel in the land.

Third, how does the command for the Jews to divorce their foreign spouses correlate with the fact that God hates divorce (see Malachi 2:16)? Ezra does not establish the norm but deals with a special case in history. It seems to have been decided that the lesser wrong of divorce would be preferable to the greater wrong of the Jewish race being polluted by intermarriage so that the messianic line of David would not be ended by being mingled with Gentiles. To solve the problem this way magnifies the mercy of God, in that the only other solution would have been to kill all those involved.

THE BOOK OF NEHEMIAH

Nehemiah was a famous cupbearer who never appears in Scripture outside of this book. As with the book of Ezra, the book recounts selected events of his leadership and was thus titled after him. Both the Greek Septuagint (LXX) and the Latin Vulgate named this book Second Ezra. Even though the two books are separate in most English Bibles, they may have once been joined together in a single unit (as currently in the Hebrew texts).

AUTHOR AND DATE

Though much of this book was clearly drawn from Nehemiah's personal diaries, both Jewish and Christian traditions recognize Ezra as the author. This is based on the evidence that Ezra and Nehemiah were originally one book and on internal evidence, such as the recurrent "hand of the Lord" theme, that dominates both books.

The events depicted in the opening chapter of Nehemiah began late in the year 446 BC, the twentieth year of Persian King Artaxerxes' reign. The book follows chronologically from Nehemiah's first term as governor of Jerusalem (c. 445–433 BC) to his second term, which possibly began in 424 BC. Ezra would have written Nehemiah sometime during or after Nehemiah's second term, but no later than 400 BC.

BACKGROUND AND SETTING

The book of Nehemiah chronicles the third return of the exiles to rebuild the wall around Jerusalem. At that time, the Persian Empire's administration of Judah, though done with a loose hand, was mindful of disruptions or any signs of rebellion from its vassals. Rebuilding the walls of conquered cities posed the most glaring threat to the Persian central administration, and only a confidant of the king could be trusted for such an operation. At the most critical juncture in Judah's revitalization, God raised up Nehemiah to fulfill this role for His people.

Several historical notes are of interest. First, Esther was Artaxerxes' stepmother, and thus could have influenced him to look favorably on the Jews. Second, Daniel's prophetic "seventy weeks" began with Artaxerxes' decree in 445 BC. Third, Egyptian documents dated to the late fifth century BC support the account of Nehemiah by mentioning Sanballat being governor of Samaria and Nehemiah being replaced as governor of Jerusalem by Bigvai. Finally, Nehemiah and Malachi represent the last of the Old Testament canonical writings, both in terms of the time the events occurred and when they were recorded.

HISTORICAL AND THEOLOGICAL THEMES

A constant theme of Nehemiah is the people's need to be diligent in reading God's Word in order to perform His will. The spiritual revival came in response to Ezra's reading of "the Book of the Law of Moses" (8:1), after which Ezra carefully explained its meaning to the people. So deep was the concern to abide by God's revealed will that the leaders took "a curse and an oath to walk in God's Law" (10:29). When the marriage reforms were carried out, they acted in accordance with that which "they read from the Book of Moses" (13:1).

A second theme involves the methods God used to bring His people back into obedience. He worked through Nehemiah's obedience, but also worked through the wicked hearts of His people's enemies. Those enemies failed not so much as a result of the success of Nehemiah's strategies but because God brought their plots to nothing. God used the opposition of Judah's enemies to drive His people to their knees in the same way that He used the favor of Cyrus to return His people to the land.

A third theme is the people's opposition. Judah's enemies started rumors that God's people had revolted against Persia, with the goal of intimidating the people into stopping reconstruction of the Jerusalem walls. However, in spite of opposition from without and heartbreaking corruption and dissension from within, the people completed the walls in only fifty-two days, experienced revival after the reading of the law by Ezra, and celebrated the Feast of Tabernacles (c. 445 BC).

INTERPRETIVE CHALLENGES

There are a number of interpretive challenges in the book of Nehemiah. First, because much of Nehemiah is explained in relationship to Jerusalem's gates (see Nehemiah 2; 3; 8; 12), it is important to have an understanding of how those gates were laid out in the city walls (see the map "Jerusalem in Nehemiah's Time" for an orientation).

Second, it is important to note that the timeline of Nehemiah 1–12 encompassed about one year (445 BC), followed by a long gap of time (more than twenty years) before the events continue again in Nehemiah 13. (See the chart "Timetable of Events.")

Finally, it must be recognized that Nehemiah actually served two governorships in Jerusalem, the first from 445–433 BC, and the second beginning possibly in 424 BC and extending to no longer than 410 BC. During his absence the people returned to their former ways, led by the high priest Eliashib, causing Nehemiah to return and institute some needed reforms. It was during Nehemiah's absence that Malachi wrote his prophetic book indicting both priests and people for their sinful defection. Nehemiah 13 was the last portion of the Old Testament to be written.

TIMETABLE OF EVENTS

Event	Approximate Date (BC)
Judah carried to Babylon	586
Zerubbabel returns with first wave	538
Haggai and Zechariah begin to prophesy	520
Temple rebuilt	515
Reign of Ahasuerus	486–465
Ezra returns with second wave	458
Nehemiah returns with third wave	March–April 445
Nehemiah starts the wall	July–August 445
Nehemiah completes the wall	August–September 445
The wall is dedicated	September–October 445
Nehemiah serves his first term as governor	445–433
Nehemiah returns to Persia	433–424
Nehemiah serves his second term as governor	424–410

1

RETURN FROM EXILE

Ezra 1:1–11

DRAWING NEAR

What are some common distractions today that can keep people from following God's will for their lives? How does a person overcome these distractions?

_____

_____

_____

_____

THE CONTEXT

In 722 BC, God allowed the powerful Assyrian Empire to invade the kingdom of Israel, conquer all its territory, and carry its people away into slavery. The author of 2 Kings sums up the sad reason for these events: "The children of Israel had sinned against the LORD their God. . . . Therefore the LORD was very angry with Israel, and removed them from His sight" (17:7–18). A little more than a century later, in 605 BC, God allowed the Babylonians to invade Judah for the same reason and begin to take its people into captivity. About twenty years after this time, Nebuchadnezzar carried the remaining Jews into Babylonian captivity.

From an outside perspective, it appeared that God's people would be forever lost to history. Yet these events did not take God by surprise—nor did they occur without warning. Furthermore, in spite of the people's sins, Jeremiah prophesied the Jews would remain in captivity for only *seventy* years. God said, "This whole land shall be a desolation and an astonishment, and these nations shall serve the king of Babylon seventy years. Then it will come to pass, when seventy years are completed, that I will punish the king of Babylon and that nation, the land of the Chaldeans, for their iniquity" (Jeremiah 25:11–12).

This study opens at the end of this seventy-year period, when God promised that His chosen people would begin to return to Jerusalem to rebuild His chosen city. However, by this time the mighty empire of Babylon had collapsed and been absorbed by another powerful empire: Persia, under the reign of Cyrus "the Great." The year was 538 BC.

KEYS TO THE TEXT

The author of Chronicles (who most likely was Ezra) provides some background information on why the Jewish people were exiled. Read his words in 2 Chronicles 36:11–21, noting the key words and phrases indicated below.

> THE LAST KING OF JUDAH: *Our studies open with a look back at the Babylonian invasion of Judah—and the events leading up to it.*

36:11. ZEDEKIAH WAS TWENTY-ONE: Zedekiah became king in Judah around 597 BC. He was the last king of Judah and ended a succession of wicked leaders. The nation of Israel had been divided into two kingdoms (Israel and Judah) after the reign of Solomon hundreds of years earlier. As mentioned in the introduction to this study, Israel had long since gone into captivity.

12. HE DID EVIL IN THE SIGHT OF THE LORD: Many of the kings of Judah—and most of the kings of Israel—had led God's people away from His Word into idolatry. The Lord had warned the Jews repeatedly that He would send them into captivity if they worshiped false gods.

JEREMIAH THE PROPHET: Jeremiah wrote the book of Lamentations to mourn the destruction of the temple, which occurred when Zedekiah was king (586 BC).

13. KING NEBUCHADNEZZAR: Nebuchadnezzar was the king of Babylon at this time. Under his leadership, the empire grew to its greatest extent.

14. ALL THE ABOMINATIONS OF THE NATIONS: These abominations included idolatry, child sacrifice, sexual perversion, denial of God as the Creator, and many more sins. All these pagan practices are abundant in modern Western society.

DEFILED THE HOUSE OF THE LORD: God's people had defiled His temple by incorporating pagan practices into their worship. This resulted in the Lord's swift judgment.

GOD'S FAITHFULNESS: *The people of Judah have been constantly unfaithful to the Lord, but God has proven completely faithful to them—even at cost to Himself.*

15. RISING UP EARLY AND SENDING THEM: The Lord was constantly faithful to His people in spite of their unfaithfulness to Him. The figure of speech here suggests that He went out of His way to lead them back to Him, going to great lengths—and at immense cost—by sending prophets again and again to urge Israel and Judah to obey His Word.

BECAUSE HE HAD COMPASSION ON HIS PEOPLE: Here we learn why God went to such lengths to turn His people back to Him: because He loved them! We will see more of God's compassion in the events leading up to the people's return to Jerusalem and find that His hand of discipline was always tempered with grace. Yet His compassion is most clearly expressed in the life and person of Jesus Christ. God sent His only Son expressly to die for our sins—and there can be no greater expression of love than that.

16. MOCKED . . . DESPISED . . . SCOFFED AT: The world has always treated the things of God with contempt, and still does today, but God's own people committed this sin. It was this contempt that ultimately brought His discipline on the nation of Judah.

17. THE KING OF THE CHALDEANS: This king is Nebuchadnezzar. Chaldea had been absorbed into the Babylonian Empire, yet the empire was interchangeably referred to by both names.

19. BURNED THE HOUSE OF GOD, BROKE DOWN THE WALL OF JERU-
SALEM: In 597 BC, King Nebuchadnezzar carried 10,000 people into captivity
from Judah, including the prophet Ezekiel. (He had actually carried captives
away from Judah in several waves, beginning in 605 BC.) Zerubbabel and Ezra
would later lead people back to Jerusalem to begin rebuilding the temple, and
Nehemiah would lead the work of rebuilding the city walls.

20. UNTIL THE RULE OF THE KINGDOM OF PERSIA: Cyrus the Great
conquered Babylon in 539 BC. He allowed Jews to begin returning to Jerusalem
the following year.

21. UNTIL THE LAND HAD ENJOYED HER SABBATHS: The Lord had commanded His people to allow their land to lie fallow every seven years. On this
seventh year, they were to neither plant crops nor reap (see Leviticus 25:4–5).
Evidently, they had failed to obey this command beginning around the time
when Eli was high priest (c. 1107–1067 BC). The Lord had warned the Jews that
He would enforce the Sabbath rest on His Promised Land if they failed to keep
it (see Leviticus 26:27–46). Jeremiah later prophesied that the people would remain in captivity for seventy years—one year for every Sabbath they neglected
(see Jeremiah 25:1–11). The exact number of Sabbath years was 490 years, the
period from Saul to the Babylonian captivity.

Read Ezra 1:1–11, noting the key words and phrases indicated below.

THE PROCLAMATION: *Seventy years later, the Lord raises up a
Gentile leader—Cyrus, the king of the Persian Empire—who will
begin to send the Jews back home.*

1:1. IN THE FIRST YEAR OF CYRUS: The Lord had prophesied through
Isaiah, saying of Cyrus, "He is My shepherd . . . saying to Jerusalem, 'You shall
be built,' and to the temple, 'Your foundation shall be laid'" (44:28). These
events occurred c. 538 BC.

BY THE MOUTH OF JEREMIAH: As previously mentioned, Jeremiah had
prophesied the return of the exiles after a seventy-year captivity in Babylon.
This period of exile likely began during the fourth year of the reign of King
Jehoiakim of Judah, c. 605 BC, when Jerusalem was captured and the temple
treasures were taken. It ended with the decree of Cyrus to allow the Jews to
return, thus spanning a period from 605/604 BC to 536/535 BC.

THE LORD STIRRED UP THE SPIRIT OF CYRUS: Throughout these studies, we will see how God used the deeds of men—both good and evil—to accomplish His sovereign purposes. Even when the circumstances seemed dark and hopeless, He was still in control and was still working out His promises for His people.

MADE A PROCLAMATION: This was the most common form of public communication and usually came from the central administration. The king would dispatch a herald, perhaps carrying a written document, into a particular city. The messenger would address the people by either going to the city gate (where people often congregated for social discourse) or gathering the crowds together in a square, occasionally by the blowing of a horn. The herald would then read the proclamation. In 1879, archaeologists recovered one such document called the Cyrus Cylinder, which was evidently some sort of general policy from Cyrus that commissioned people from many lands to return to their cities to rebuild the temples to their gods. Whether or not this document was an extension of the proclamation made to the Jewish exiles in this passage must remain a matter of speculation.

2. THE LORD GOD OF HEAVEN HAS GIVEN ME: Cyrus evidently recognized the sovereign hand of God in his life. He acknowledged that he himself held power in Persia only because the Lord had given it to him—even though he probably did not worship Yahweh as the only true God. Josephus, a Jewish historian, would later write that Daniel was Cyrus's prime minister and that he read prophecies to the king that mentioned Cyrus by name—more than a century before Cyrus was born (see Isaiah 44:28). According to Josephus, this led Cyrus to make his decree allowing the Jews to return to Jerusalem.

TO BUILD HIM A HOUSE: This refers to the second temple, which the Jews would begin to build after they returned to Jerusalem in the first wave led by Zerubbabel. During the first century AD, King Herod would commission a massive reconstruction effort in which he greatly expanded the temple mount. This second temple would stand until 70 AD, when, after the people rebelled, the Roman general Titus seized the city and destroyed the structure.

4. LET THE MEN OF HIS PLACE HELP HIM: Cyrus commanded the neighbors of the returning Jews to assist them with finances and goods for their trip and for the work of rebuilding the temple. This was reminiscent of the Israelites' preparations for the exodus from Egypt, when the Lord had them ask their neighbors for gold, silver, and clothing (see Exodus 12:35–36).

THE EXILES RETURN: In response to Cyrus's proclamation, many of the Jewish exiles decide to return to Jerusalem. It will not turn out to be a simple endeavor.

5. ALL WHOSE SPIRITS GOD HAD MOVED: The Hebrew word here literally means "to rouse up or awaken," and it is the same expression used of Cyrus in verse 1. The Lord stirred the hearts of His people and made many of them restless and unsettled with the knowledge that His temple was lying in ruins back in Judah. The Jews were not enslaved in Persia but were permitted to live as all other Persians lived, and many of them had risen to prosperity and influence. It is possible, therefore, that God's people had become comfortable and complacent with their lot, so the Lord stirred their hearts to be grieved over the desecration of His holy temple and His chosen city. The important thing to note, however, is that God motivated and directed this work of rebuilding, not men or any one charismatic leader. "Unless the LORD builds the house, they labor in vain who build it" (Psalm 127:1).

6. ALL THAT WAS WILLINGLY OFFERED: Throughout the books of Ezra and Nehemiah we find many parallels to the story of the Exodus. One can hear faint echoes of the Egyptians supplying treasures in order to provide splendor for the tabernacle (see Exodus 11:2). However, the Jews there had been slaves, and the Egyptians had despised them, so the Israelites "plundered the Egyptians" (Exodus 12:36). But in this case there is a hint of goodwill involved, which suggests the Jews' fellow countrymen were glad to assist them in rebuilding the Lord's house. Other nations around Israel were called to contribute as well. They were also assisted by some of their captive countrymen who had been born in Babylon and chose to remain, and perhaps by some Babylonians and Assyrians who were favorably disposed to Cyrus or the Jews.

7. THE ARTICLES OF THE HOUSE OF THE LORD: These were the vessels that Nebuchadnezzar had removed when he sacked the temple (see 2 Kings 24:13) God had preserved them with the Babylonians for the Jewish people's return as prophesied by Jeremiah (see 27:22).

8. SHESHBAZZAR THE PRINCE OF JUDAH: Nothing else is said about this man in the Bible, but most likely he was a political appointee of Cyrus to oversee Judah. He is not to be confused with Zerubbabel, who was the leader recognized by the Jews and by the Lord. While Zerubbabel did not serve as king, he was in the Davidic line of the Messiah (see Matthew 1:12).

9. THIS IS THE NUMBER OF THEM: The 2,499 articles counted in verses 9 and 10 are representative of the total of 5,400 mentioned in verse 11.

11. THE CAPTIVES WHO WERE BROUGHT: These were the individuals King Nebuchadnezzar had taken into Babylonian captivity from Jerusalem, and their return probably occurred early during the reign of Cyrus (c. 538/537 BC). The journey from Babylon to Jerusalem would have taken three to five months.

UNLEASHING THE TEXT

1) Why did God send the Jews into captivity? Why did He limit the time of their captivity to seventy years?

_____

_____

_____

_____

2) How had God's people drifted away from Him into idolatry? What contributed to their sin? What did God do to turn them back to Himself?

_____

_____

_____

_____

3) In what ways did God show compassion to the Jews over the centuries? In what ways was He showing compassion by sending them into captivity?

_____

_____

_____

_____

4) What does Ezra mean when he says the Lord "stirred up" the hearts of the Jews? Why was this needed? What was God trying to accomplish?

_____

_____

_____

EXPLORING THE MEANING

God keeps all His promises. God had promised His people, "If you diligently obey the voice of the LORD your God, to observe carefully all His commandments which I command you today, that the LORD your God will set you high above all nations of the earth" (Deuteronomy 28:1). Under the reign of David, the nation of Israel obeyed the Lord's commands, and God kept that promise, subduing all the nation's enemies and giving Israel peace and prosperity. But God had made another promise in that same passage: "But it shall come to pass, if you do not obey the voice of the LORD your God . . . you shall beget sons and daughters, but they shall not be yours; for they shall go into captivity" (verses 15, 41).

Beginning with the reign of King Solomon and extending until the time of the exile, the nation's kings gradually led God's people away from obedience and into idolatry. As a result, God proved faithful to His second promise and sent them into captivity. However, when this time came, the Lord then promised His people that they would return to Jerusalem in seventy years—and He kept that promise as well. He first raised up Nebuchadnezzar to carry the nation into Babylon, and then He raised up Cyrus to absorb Babylon into Persia and set His people free. He holds sovereign control over all human affairs, and He can raise up an empire or throw it down as He sees fit. But whatever happens, He always keeps His promises.

God has not changed since the time of Ezra. He has given many promises to Christians, both of blessing and of discipline, and He still keeps those promises. One of the most important promises of all is this: "For God so loved the world that He gave His only begotten Son, that whoever believes in Him should not perish but have everlasting life. For God did not send His Son into the world to condemn the world, but that the world through Him might be saved. He who believes in Him is not condemned; but he who does not believe is condemned already, because he has not believed in the name of the only begotten Son of God" (John 3:16–18). God will keep this promise of eternal life to anyone who accepts Jesus, but He will also keep His promise of eternal judgment for anyone who rejects Christ. If you do not know Jesus as your Savior, claim God's promise of salvation right now—because God keeps *all* His promises.

The Lord sends discipline to help us, not to harm us. The Lord sent the Babylonian army into Judah to carry His people into captivity when they turned away from Him and pursued nonexistent pagan gods. But two factors in this are important for us to remember. First, the people had been unfaithful to God for centuries (with brief periods of revival during that time), which demonstrates God's great patience and grace. Second, the Lord sent the Jews into captivity to discipline them and turn them back to Himself, *not* to destroy them. This was a loving but stern Father's hand of correction, not a harsh judge's verdict of condemnation.

The author of Chronicles made it clear that the Lord had patiently endured hundreds of years of disobedience in His people, "rising up early and sending" His prophets to remind them of His Word again and again, "because He had compassion on His people and on His dwelling place" (2 Chronicles 36:15). Even in the midst of discipline, the Lord demonstrated His compassion and love by raising up a new king who would send His people back to Jerusalem and by restricting the captivity to a relatively short period of time. Jeremiah prophesied concerning this time: "For thus says the Lord: After seventy years are completed at Babylon, I will visit you and perform My good word toward you, and cause you to return to this place. For I know the thoughts that I think toward you, says the Lord, thoughts of peace and not of evil, to give you a future and a hope" (29:10–11).

The whole reason the Lord sent His people into captivity was to turn their hearts back to Him. "Then you will call upon Me and go and pray to Me," He said, "and I will listen to you. And you will seek Me and find Me, when you search for Me with all your heart" (verses 12–13). His ways have not changed today. The Lord may send discipline into our lives, but He does so in order to draw us toward Himself—not to push us away. When hardship enters our lives, we seek His face, and He has promised that we will find Him.

This world is not our home. The people of Judah had been carried away to captivity, but they had not been made slaves as they were many centuries before in Egypt. Instead, they were allowed to establish relatively normal lives within the new land, and many of the Jews had risen to levels of power and prosperity. Daniel, for example, served at least three different kings as a close personal counselor. Yet this relative freedom brought a danger the Israelites had not faced when they were slaves: *complacency.* Many of God's people had become quite comfortable in captivity and were fitting in to the society and doing well.

The problem was that God did not intend for His people to make their permanent home outside of Judah. Their real home was there, and the Lord did not want them to put down roots anywhere else. God's temple in Jerusalem was in ruins, the city's walls lay in rubble, and the Lord grieved over that situation. He wanted His people to share His priorities and to long to return to their proper land where they would worship and serve Him as He had ordained. The world in which they had grown so content was *not* their home.

This is equally true for Christians today. This world is not our home! It is not wrong to pursue a career or to establish a home, but the Lord does not want us to lose our eternal focus. He wants us to remember that the things of eternity are what matter most, not the things of this world. Paul wrote, "Set your mind on things above, not on things on the earth. For you died, and your life is hidden with Christ in God" (Colossians 3:2–3). Paul was reminding us that by being born again into the salvation of Christ, we have died to the things of this world. And if we are dead to this world, there is no purpose in trying to make our home here. Our existence is with Christ in eternity, and that is where our focus needs to remain.

REFLECTING ON THE TEXT

5) What promises did God keep in these passages? What part did the behavior and attitudes of the Jews play in God's promises?

_____

_____

_____

6) Why did God choose to use Nebuchadnezzar and Cyrus to fulfill His plans? What does this suggest about His sovereignty?

_____

_____

_____

_____

7) Why did God need to "rouse" the hearts of His people to return to Jerusalem? What worldly elements tend to lull Christians into complacency?

_____

_____

_____

_____

8) When has the Lord sent discipline into your life? What was He trying to accomplish? How did you respond to that discipline?

_____

_____

_____

_____

PERSONAL RESPONSE

9) Have you accepted Jesus as your Lord and Savior and know that you will see the eternal home He has prepared for you? If not, what is preventing you from doing so right now?

_____

_____

_____

10) What might the Lord be "stirring up" your heart to do at present? What things of this world might be distracting you from sharing His priorities?

_____

_____

_____

2

THE WORK BEGINS

Ezra 2:1–3:13

DRAWING NEAR

What are some of the things that get in the way of people setting the right priorities? In what ways are Christians often guilty of not setting the priorities that God wants them to set?

_____

_____

_____

THE CONTEXT

During the exodus from Egypt, the Lord demonstrated His presence with His people in a variety of tangible ways. He showed that He was with them by providing heavy cloud cover during the day to shield the people from the desert sun. By night, He provided a dramatic pillar of fire to illuminate the darkness. Beyond these manifestations, the Lord also commanded the people to construct a portable temple, which they were to set up whenever they made camp. At the center of this tabernacle was the ark of the covenant.

The ark represented God's chosen place of meeting with His people—a physical manifestation of His presence wherever they went. Many generations later, King Solomon built a magnificent permanent temple in Jerusalem to house the ark, and this became the Lord's chosen place for His people to assemble for corporate worship. After the nation split, Jeroboam set up alternate sites of worship in the north—where he set up calves made of gold—but the true site of the Lord's worship remained in Jerusalem in the south. The first temple existed until King Nebuchadnezzar conquered the land and carried the Jews into captivity. At that time he destroyed that temple and absconded with the ark.

In this study, the Jews have returned to Jerusalem from exile, and it is time for them to begin work on rebuilding the temple. They gather together as one—but then, instead of starting the work on the actual temple, they rebuild the altar that will go *inside* the temple. At first glance this might seem like building one's living room furniture before building the house, but in reality it demonstrates a correct order of priorities in God's prescribed worship. We will discover that even without the ark of the covenant, God was still with His people—because it is people who comprise God's ultimate temple, not a building made of bricks and mortar.

KEYS TO THE TEXT

Read Ezra 2:1–3:13, noting the key words and phrases indicated below.

> COUNTING THE CAPTIVES: *Ezra's chronicle of the Jewish exiles' return under Zerubbabel begins with a comprehensive listing of the people who made the journey.*

2:1. WHO CAME BACK FROM THE CAPTIVITY: This list is given almost identically in Nehemiah 7:6–73. The "province" refers to Judah, which by this time had been reduced from an illustrious, independent, and powerful kingdom to an obscure servile province of the Persian Empire. The returning Jews were still considered subjects of Cyrus living in a Persian province.

2. THOSE WHO CAME WITH ZERUBBABEL: As previously mentioned, this man was the rightful leader of Judah in that he was of the lineage of David through Jehoiachin (see 1 Chronicles 3:17–19). His name means "offspring of Babylon," which indicated his place of birth. Zerubbabel, rather than Cyrus's political appointee Sheshbazzar, led Judah according to God's will.

JESHUA: The high priest of the first return, whose name means "Jehovah saves," was called *Joshua* in Haggai 1:1 and Zechariah 3:1. His father, Jozadak, had been among those taken into exile. He came from the lineage of Levi, Aaron, Eleazar, and Phinehas, and thus was legitimately in the line of the high priest (see Numbers 25:10–13).

NEHEMIAH . . . MORDECAI: These were not the same men listed in Nehemiah or Esther.

3. THE PEOPLE OF PAROSH: Ezra lists various Jewish families in verses 3 to 20 who were part of what would be known as the "first wave" of Jewish exiles returning to Jerusalem.

21. THE PEOPLE OF BETHLEHEM: Ezra lists returning exiles from various Judean cities in verses 21 to 35.

36. THE PRIESTS: The record of the priests and Levites in Nehemiah 12:1–9 lists three generations of high priests beginning with Jeshua. Ezra lists priests and Levites in verses 36 to 42.

43. THE NETHINIM: These were temple servants—the descendants of the Gibeonites who performed servile duties at the temple. Ezra lists them in verses 43 to 54.

55. THE SONS OF SOLOMON'S SERVANTS: These are the descendants of Solomon's servants, whom Ezra lists in verses 55 to 57.

59. AND THESE WERE THE ONES: In verses 59 to 62, Ezra lists several families whose genealogical information could not be verified.

63. CONSULT WITH THE URIM AND THUMMIM: Because these people's lineage could not be determined, they were banned from priesthood and could not "eat of the most holy things" until a priest could consult with the Urim and Thummim. These objects, kept in the breastplate of the high priest, were used to determine God's will. "You shall put in the breastplate of judgment the Urim and the Thummim, and they shall be over Aaron's heart when he goes in before the LORD" (Exodus 28:30).

64. THE WHOLE ASSEMBLY TOGETHER: The number of returning exiles listed here is 12,000 more than the particular numbers given in the catalog, when added together. Reckoning up the smaller numbers, they amount to 29,818 in Ezra 2 and to 31,089 in the parallel chapter in Nehemiah 7. Ezra also mentions 494 persons omitted by Nehemiah, and Nehemiah mentions 1,765 not noticed by Ezra. If Ezra's surplus is added to the sum in Nehemiah, and Nehemiah's surplus to the number in Ezra, they both become 31,583. Subtracting

this from 42,360, there is a deficiency of 10,777. These were omitted because they did not belong to Judah or Benjamin or to the priests, but to the other tribes. The servants and singers, male and female, were reckoned separately so that, putting all of them together, the number of all who went with Zerubbabel amounted to 50,000, with 8,000 beasts of burden.

69. GOLD DRACHMAS . . . MINAS OF SILVER: Drachma probably refers to a Persian coin, the *daric*, named after Darius I. This quantity would have amounted to approximately 1,100 pounds of gold. A mina weighed about one and one-quarter pounds, so this would represent three tons of silver.

> BUILDING THE ALTAR: *The returning Jews soon gather in Jerusalem, where they will rebuild the temple. However, they begin the project by first building the altar.*

3:1. THE SEVENTH MONTH: After the Jews' arrival in their homeland, they were at first occupied with their own dwellings in and around Jerusalem, but after that work was done, they turned to building the altar of burnt offering. In the "seventh month" (September–October 537 BC), the Jews celebrated three important annual observances: the Feast of Trumpets, the Day of Atonement, and the Feast of Tabernacles (see Numbers 29:1–38). Such an assembly had not convened for seventy years. More than ninety years later, Nehemiah and Ezra would lead a similar celebration (see Nehemiah 8:13–18).

THE PEOPLE GATHERED TOGETHER AS ONE MAN: This refers again to the people who had chosen to return to Jerusalem. Their unity of purpose here demonstrated that they were deeply concerned with restoring the forms of worship that the Lord had commanded under Moses. It also suggests that the Spirit of God was at work in their hearts, stirring them up to obedience just as He had done with Cyrus and others in Ezra 1:5.

2. THEN JESHUA . . . AND ZERUBBABEL: It is significant that these two important men—Jeshua, the high priest, and Zerubbabel, the head of the tribe of Judah—led the Jews in returning to Jerusalem. The kings and priests of Judah and Israel had previously led the people *away* from God, but now the nation's leaders, both at the civic and spiritual levels, were leading the people *back* to obedience to His Word.

BUILT THE ALTAR OF THE GOD OF ISRAEL: It is also significant that the people's first act of rebuilding was the altar rather than the temple or the city walls. This demonstrated that the returning exiles' first priority was in offering sacrifices and repenting of their sins, and that this took precedence over any other act of worship (and even over their own physical safety). The people were trusting God to protect them while they obeyed His commands.

3. FEAR HAD COME UPON THEM: The settlers who had come to occupy the land during the seventy years of Israel's absence were deportees brought in from other countries by the Assyrians and the Babylonians. They saw the returning Jews as a tremendous threat to their possessions, land, and way of life, for they viewed the land as their own by right of seventy years of occupation, while the Jews viewed it as theirs by virtue of God's command. We can still see this conflict occurring in the Middle East today.

SET THE ALTAR: This was all that was needed to reestablish temple worship. The people reset it on its old foundation (or *bases*) so it occupied its sacred site. The burnt offerings they sacrificed to God were the most common offerings for sin.

> LAYING THE FOUNDATION: *Having established obedience to God's Word, the people now turn their attention to the mechanics of building the temple.*

4. THE FEAST OF TABERNACLES: This festival, also called the Feast of Booths, commemorated the Israelites' wandering in the wilderness during their exodus from Egypt (see Leviticus 23:33–43).

5. A FREEWILL OFFERING TO THE LORD: In addition to reinstituting the sacrifices and feasts that God had commanded, the people began to offer voluntary tithes—all prior to rebuilding the temple. This demonstrated that worship of the Lord consists of confession and repentance of sins, worship, and giving—but not meeting inside a building. The building came later, but only after proper worship and obedience had been reestablished.

6. THE FOUNDATION OF THE TEMPLE OF THE LORD HAD NOT BEEN LAID: In a spiritual sense, the people were laying a firm foundation for the temple by obeying God's Word. Obedience is more important to God's church than bricks and mortar.

7. THEY ALSO GAVE MONEY TO THE MASONS AND THE CARPENTERS: The process of rebuilding the temple is similar to the original construction under Solomon (see 1 Kings 5–6). The Jews gave freely of their possessions, time,

and skills to the construction and paid laborers and manufacturers the proper rates. Note that they did not ask foreigners to donate. The Jews would have accepted those gifts if offered, but they did not expect that of foreigners, nor did they try to get things for free. As David said, "I will not take what is yours for the LORD, nor offer burnt offerings with that which costs me nothing" (1 Chronicles 21:24).

PEOPLE OF SIDON AND TYRE . . . CEDAR LOGS FROM LEBANON . . . TO JOPPA: The workmen loaded cedar logs onto ships in the cities of Tyre and Sidon to the north, on the coast of the Mediterranean (or Great Sea), and then sailed them south to the city of Joppa, which was approximately forty miles from Jerusalem.

8. IN THE SECOND MONTH OF THE SECOND YEAR: That is April–May 536 BC. This officially ended the seventy-year captivity that began in 605 BC. Once again, we see that construction of the temple did not even begin until all the elements of obedience and worship were in place.

WEEPING AND REJOICING: The people gather in unity and respond to the preliminary construction—some with weeping, and others with shouts of joy.

ALL THOSE WHO HAD COME OUT OF THE CAPTIVITY: Once again, we see the unity and wholeheartedness of God's people. They joined together as one to participate in the building of the temple, just as they had shown unity in obedience.

11. THEY SANG RESPONSIVELY: This song of praise is evidently from Psalm 136:1. The priests might have sung, "Oh, give thanks to the LORD," and then one group of the people would have responded with the words, "For He is good!" The second group would then respond, "For His mercy endures forever toward Israel."

12. OLD MEN . . . WEPT WITH A LOUD VOICE: These old men had been young when carried into captivity. They would have remembered Solomon's glorious temple that stood in Jerusalem at the time. They grieved over the lost splendor of Solomon's structure, for this second temple did not begin to match the grandeur of the first temple, nor did the presence of God reside within it. It was apparent that the new nation was small and weak—and that the new temple was smaller and less beautiful by far. Gone were all the riches and glory

as in the days of David and Solomon. However, most of all, the old men wept over the fact that the ark of the covenant was gone, and with it the manifestation of the Lord's presence.

YET MANY SHOUTED ALOUD FOR JOY: However, in spite of the loss of the ark, many of the people recognized that God was still with His people—which alone was cause for joyful shouting and praise (see Zechariah 4:7–10). It is possible that Psalm 126 was written for this occasion and sung at the celebration.

13. THE SOUND WAS HEARD AFAR OFF: The obedient praise and worship of God's people carries a profound testimony to the world around us. It draws people toward the Lord just as curiosity might have drawn neighboring people toward Jerusalem on this day.

UNLEASHING THE TEXT

1) Why does this passage reiterate that the people gathered "as one man" (Ezra 3:1)? What does this indicate? What drew the people together?

_____

_____

_____

2) Why did the returning exiles build the altar before the temple that would house it? Why did they build it before they constructed the city walls that would protect them? What does this indicate they knew about God's priorities?

_____

_____

_____

_____

3) Why had fear come on the people (see Ezra 3:3)? What did this have to do with rebuilding the altar?

_____

_____

_____

4) What was involved in the actual building of the temple? What roles did the people play in the process? What did the construction cost them?

_____

_____

_____

EXPLORING THE MEANING

God dwells in believers, not in a temple. Cyrus the Great of Persia allowed the Jews to return to Jerusalem for the express purpose of rebuilding the Lord's temple there. However, as we have seen in this study, the people did not immediately turn their attention to that particular construction project. Rather, the first thing they did was rebuild the altar—even though that altar would eventually be housed within the temple. Their top priority was being personally and corporately obedient to God's Word, not constructing a building in which to worship.

The people's priorities demonstrated that they understood God's priorities. They knew that "to obey is better than sacrifice, and to heed [God's Word] than the fat of rams" (1 Samuel 15:22). Yet in those days the temple represented the Lord's presence, and its completion was important to the proper worship by His people. This emphasis on personal and corporate sacrifice underscored the fact that the Lord is more concerned with our obedience than with our outward shows of worship.

When Jesus was crucified, God abolished the need for the temple in Jerusalem. He tore the curtain that separated the Most Holy from His people to demonstrate that His presence would no longer be found inside a building. God's presence now resides in the very people who belong to Him, because God has reconciled them to Himself through their faith in Jesus Christ. God said this to John in the book of Revelation: "Behold, the tabernacle of God is with men, and He will dwell with them, and they shall be His people. God Himself will be with them and be their God" (21:3). There is no longer a need for a temple simply because *we* are His temple!

God's people are unified through their obedience. The devil seeks to divide believers. He works ceaselessly to separate what God has brought together, whether that is marriages, churches, or any other relationship in which unity and commitment are essential. Ironically, the devil also works tirelessly to *remove* separations and divisions that God has established: right from wrong, darkness from light, good from evil . . . and on and on. The evil one's goal is to create unity in wickedness and disunity in righteousness.

It is interesting to note that the nations of Israel and Judah were fairly unified in pursuing wickedness for many generations. This was the sort of unity that the devil breeds, not the unity that God requires. The Lord calls His people to be unified in obedience. When we pursue disobedience, or when we allow disunity to separate Christians, we are following the paths of wickedness rather than the ways of righteousness.

The exiles who returned to Jerusalem drew together with one accord. They all worked together as one to reestablish godly worship—and the Lord blessed their efforts tremendously. We will see clearly as we go through these studies how the Lord stymied the efforts of others who sought to disrupt His work and how He preserved and blessed His people as they did that work. When Christians unite in obedience to God's Word, nothing can stand in their way.

The Lord will put an end to mourning. When the returning exiles laid the foundation for the temple in Jerusalem, there was a mixed response from the people. Many shouted with joy at seeing the Lord rebuilding what had been utterly destroyed. At the same time, many others wept with deep grief over their memories of what had once been. Ironically, both responses were valid—but in the long run, the joyful shouting drowned out the tears.

The people of Israel had good reason to mourn, because it was their own sin and stubbornness that had led to the destruction of the temple and the loss of all it contained—including the ark of the covenant. Yet God had not abandoned His people, and He had not forgotten His promises of faithfulness and blessing. The Lord was still at work, and what mattered most was that Israel still existed, due to the promise of God. Tears had a place, but the shouts of joy would last far longer.

When we sin, we often do grave damage to ourselves and to others. We do well when we grieve and mourn over our own sinful behavior. We also do well when we repent and recognize the depth of the damage we have caused. But we must also remember that God has not abandoned us, even in the midst of deliberate sin. He may choose to bring discipline into our lives to urge us toward repentance, but He will never forsake us and will never disinherit those who are His children through the redemption of Jesus Christ. In the eternal kingdom, "God will wipe away every tear from their eyes; there shall be no more death, nor sorrow, nor crying. There shall be no more pain, for the former things have passed away" (Revelation 21:4).

REFLECTING ON THE TEXT

5) Why did some people shout with joy when the foundation was laid? Why did others weep? If you had been there, how do you think you would have responded?

_____

_____

_____

6) How would you have reacted if you had been outside Jerusalem at the time of this loud shouting? How does your worship of God influence the people around you?

_____

_____

_____

7) Why was unity among the people so important to the effort to rebuild the temple? In what ways today is unity among Christians important?

_____

_____

_____

_____

8) What did the apostle Paul mean when he said a Christian is "the temple of God" (1 Corinthians 3:16)? What implication does this have in your life?

_____

_____

_____

_____

PERSONAL RESPONSE

9) When have you grieved over your past sins? When have you rejoiced over God's faithfulness and blessings? When has God turned your tears into joy?

_____

_____

_____

_____

_____

10) Which takes higher priority in your life: personal obedience to God's Word or regular attendance at church? Which is God's higher priority?

_____

_____

_____

_____

3

TROUBLE WITH SAMARITANS
Ezra 4:1–5:17

DRAWING NEAR

What are some famous deals—whether in business, politics, or other—that seemed good on the surface but in the end proved to be disastrous to one of the parties?

_____

_____

_____

THE CONTEXT

As previously mentioned, in 722 BC the Assyrian king Shalmaneser V invaded the northern kingdom of Israel and quickly conquered the land. However, the people in the capital city of Samaria—due to the city's strong walls, internal water supply, and storehouses of food—were able to resist the Assyrian attack for three years. When the city finally fell and the people were carried away, the Assyrians repopulated the area with people from other lands they had conquered. Those foreigners settled in Samaria and intermarried with the few Israelites who were still living there, and their descendants became known as Samaritans.

These Samaritans did not fear God and, as a result, the Bible tells us that as a form of discipline, "the LORD sent lions among them, which killed some of them" (2 Kings 17:25). The people recognized this as the hand of God, but they thought He was only the God of Samaria—they did not understand that His control extended to the entire world. So the Lord sent a priest to live with them, and he "taught them how they should fear the LORD" (verse 28). The Samaritans embraced the worship rituals the priest taught, but they did not forsake their other gods. They believed they could simply add the God of all creation to their long list of idols, and so invented their own syncretistic religious practices.

When Zerubbabel and the people of Judah returned to Jerusalem, they discovered that the Samaritans were still living nearby. Soon the two groups would begin to interact—and those encounters would not lead to pleasant outcomes for the Jews. In this study, we will see what happens when obedient believers like the exiles are confronted by pious frauds.

KEYS TO THE TEXT

Read Ezra 4:1–5:17, noting the key words and phrases indicated below.

A FRIENDLY OFFER: The Samaritans, the neighbors of the Jews, come to Jerusalem and offer to help build God's temple. But the people of Judah reject the offer.

1. THE ADVERSARIES OF JUDAH AND BENJAMIN: These *adversaries* were the Samaritans. As previously noted, these foreigners had intermarried with the remaining Israelites and brought their own brands of idolatry with them.

2. WE SEEK YOUR GOD AS YOU DO: This statement was true from the Samaritans' point of view, but it was absolutely false from God's perspective. The Lord had sent a priest to Samaria to teach His truth to those who had been transported there by the Assyrians during the Israelite captivity. The people had embraced the Lord in part, thinking He was "the God of the land" (2 Kings 17:26) where they had been transported, and they wanted to appease Him. However, they had not completely forsaken their false gods in the process; rather, they had merely attempted to add the one true God to their pantheon of idols.

3. WE ALONE WILL BUILD TO THE LORD GOD OF ISRAEL: This was an important and costly decision on the part of Judah's leaders. They were not arbitrarily excluding outsiders from building the temple out of some spirit of snobbery, nor were they excluding others merely out of obedience to Cyrus's commands. Rather, they were taking a firm stand that only God's obedient worshipers were permitted to participate in building His temple, and they were avoiding contact with the very idolatry that had caused the Lord to send them into captivity in the first place. The note from Cyrus gave authority to their refusal.

SHOWING THEIR TRUE FACE: The Samaritans respond by showing their true motives and begin an ongoing attempt to stop God's work in Jerusalem.

4. TRIED TO DISCOURAGE THE PEOPLE OF JUDAH: Discouragement is one of the devil's favorite tactics in trying to thwart the work of God. His goal is to persuade God's people to give up on obedience and turn to the easier temptations of the flesh. God had previously warned His people not to give in to discouragement: "Look, the LORD your God has set the land before you; go up and possess it, as the LORD God of your fathers has spoken to you; do not fear or be discouraged" (Deuteronomy 1:21). The same warning is relevant for us today—God wants us to choose instead to trust Him for the outcome.

5. HIRED COUNSELORS AGAINST THEM: The Samaritans took some form of legal action against the Jews. They hoped to bog down the Jews in litigation if they couldn't prevent the rebuilding outright. God's enemies still use this tactic today by staging attempts to thwart the spread of the gospel through laws and lawsuits.

FRUSTRATE THEIR PURPOSE: The legal experts the Samaritans hired were successful in causing a sixteen-year delay of the rebuilding effort (c. 536–520 BC). In the meantime, the people took more interest in their personal affairs than spiritual matters (see Haggai 1:2–6). This delay lasted "all the days of Cyrus" and into the days of Darius, who ruled Persia from 521–486 BC.

6. THEY WROTE AN ACCUSATION: The Hebrew word for *accusation* here is related to the word for *Satan*. Satan is the accuser of the brethren (see Revelation 12:10) and tirelessly brings accusations against God's people. The enemies of God's people are like their father, the devil (see John 8:44), and thus persistently do the same.

7. ARTAXERXES KING OF PERSIA: Ezra chronicles some of the continued opposition the Samaritans waged against the Jewish people. The letters sent to King Artaxerxes occurred later, during the time when Nehemiah was ministering in Jerusalem. Note that two different words for *letter* are used in this passage. The first is an official document as opposed to a simple form of correspondence. The second is the generic term for letter. The context verifies the choices of two different terms, since two different letters are indicated.

10. THE GREAT AND NOBLE OSNAPPER: This probably is another name for the Assyrian king Ashurbanipal (c. 669–633 BC), who resettled Samaria with foreigners. The obsequious tone of the enemies' letter is typical of those who use flattery and attempt to ingratiate themselves to those in power in the hopes of accomplishing their own personal agendas. The Assyrians were noted for their cruelty and barbarity, and their kings were anything but "great and noble."

12. THE REBELLIOUS AND EVIL CITY: God's view of Jerusalem was quite different: "Beautiful in elevation, the joy of the whole earth, is Mount Zion on the sides of the north, the city of the great King" (Psalm 48:2). Yet this illustrates another favorite tactic of God's enemies: to accuse His people of the very wickedness that they commit themselves. As Isaiah wrote, "Woe to those who call evil good, and good evil; who put darkness for light, and light for darkness; who put bitter for sweet, and sweet for bitter!" (Isaiah 5:20).

12. THE JEWS THAT CAME UP FROM YOU: The name *Jews* for the people of God was generally used after the captivity, because the exiles who returned to the land were mainly from Judah. Most of the people of the ten northern tribes had been dispersed, and the largest number of returnees came from the two southern tribes.

SPEAKING THE KING'S LANGUAGE: The enemies of God finally find a sympathetic ear with King Artaxerxes—when they tell him that he will lose money—and he stops the work.

13. THEY WILL NOT PAY TAX, TRIBUTE, OR CUSTOM: The Samaritans told the Persian king that the Jews would not pay any taxes or tributes to him after the work on the city and its walls had been completed. Of course this was not true, yet the accusation hit a chord in the mind of King Artaxerxes. Judah had historically at times refused to pay tribute to foreign kings prior to the captivity.

THE KING'S TREASURY WILL BE DIMINISHED: Here is the crux of the Samaritans' real argument. If King Artaxerxes permitted the Jews to continue their rebuilding projects, he would end up losing money. Rulers in Ezra's day were no different from those in our own time, and this argument proved all too effective.

14. IT WAS NOT PROPER FOR US TO SEE THE KING'S DISHONOR: Here again we see the hypocrisy and dissembling of God's enemies. They pretended to have high and lofty motives, yet they were merely pursuing their own selfish gain.

15. THE BOOK OF THE RECORDS: This was an administrative document called a "memorandum" kept on file in the royal archives. The enemies of the Jews noted that in this document the king would find a record of Jerusalem's destruction by the Babylonian king Nebuchadnezzar (c. 586 BC).

19. REBELLION AND SEDITION HAVE BEEN FOSTERED IN IT: This refers to the rebellions of Kings Jehoiakim (see 2 Kings 24:1), Jehoiachin (see verses 9, 12), and Zedekiah (see verse 20)—all of whom ruled in Judah prior to the captivity. These rebellions were against Babylon, not against Persia.

19. AND I GAVE THE COMMAND: This line might better be translated, "I established a decree." In other words, this was no simple routine order given by the king to one person, but a major edict to a large group of people.

21. NOW GIVE THE COMMAND: With this decree the king called to a halt not the efforts of one or two workers but the efforts of 50,000 workers. The king was commissioning a decree of great significance, and it would not lose its authority until the king established a new decree.

23. KING ARTAXERXES' LETTER: Another official document, as opposed to a generic letter, came from Artaxerxes transferring authority to the regional leaders to establish the decree. Without the king's official administrative correspondence, the decree could not have been established.

BY FORCE OF ARMS MADE THEM CEASE: The enemies of God's people may succeed temporarily in outlawing obedience to His Word, but God is always in control and no power on earth or in hell can prevent the fulfillment of His plans. In a later study, we will see that the people of Jerusalem eventually completed the temple in spite of the efforts of their enemies.

24. THE WORK . . . CEASED, AND IT WAS DISCONTINUED: It was this decree that halted the Jews' rebuilding efforts for sixteen years.

THE WORK RESUMES: God speaks through His prophets and instructs the people to continue the work on the temple—in spite of the Persian king's decree.

5:1. HAGGAI AND ZECHARIAH: The book of Haggai is styled as a "royal administrative correspondence" sent from the Sovereign King of the universe through the "the LORD's messenger," who was Haggai (1:13). The prophet addressed part of the message specifically to Zerubbabel, the political leader, and to Joshua, the religious leader, telling them to "be strong . . . and work" on the temple because God was with them (see 2:4). This prophet, along with Zechariah, gave severe reproaches and threats to the people if they did not return to the building, but promised national prosperity if they continued the work. Not long after the exiles heard this message, the temple work began once again.

2. PROPHETS OF GOD: These men who helped in building the temple would be in addition to Haggai and Zechariah.

3. TATTENAI THE GOVERNOR: He was most likely a Persian official. He basically asked the people, "Who issued you a royal decree to build?"

5. BUT THE EYE OF THEIR GOD WAS UPON THE ELDERS: God's hand of protection, which had led this endeavor, allowed the work to continue while official communication was going on between Tattenai and Darius, the Persian king.

THE GOVERNOR'S LETTER: Tattenai reports to King Darius that the Jews are violating the official decree that is in place—but he also includes the Jewish people's response.

8. HEAVY STONES, AND TIMBER: This technique of using beams and stone blocks was a well-known form of wall construction. It appears the governor mentioned this in his letter to tell Darius that the Jews were preparing for conflict or battle. Including this piece of information would have served as a threat to the Persian king, who wanted no such conflict.

11. THEY RETURNED US AN ANSWER: In other words, the Jews sent back a report (an official document for the archives). The "great king of Israel" the people mention was Solomon, who built the first temple (c. 966–960 BC).

12. GAVE THEM INTO THE HAND OF NEBUCHADNEZZAR. This expression was used commonly in royal administrative correspondence when a more powerful administrator, such as a king, relinquished some of his authority to an underling and yet kept the lower administrative official under his command. The point here was that God—as the sovereign King of the universe—had satisfied His wrath by relinquishing the authority for this administrative action to Nebuchadnezzar. The greatest king the ancient Near East had ever known was just a petty official in the administration of the sovereign Lord.

13. IN THE FIRST YEAR OF CYRUS: This refers to the initial proclamation that Cyrus had made in Ezra 1:2–4, which initiated the Jewish people's return to Jerusalem.

16. SHESHBAZZAR CAME AND LAID THE FOUNDATION: This seems to contradict the statement in Ezra 3:8–10 that Zerubbabel, Jeshua, and the Jewish workmen laid the foundation, but in truth it does not. Sheshbazzar was the political appointee of the Persian king over the Jews, and he was thus given official credit for work actually done by them.

UNLEASHING THE TEXT

1) If you had been present when the Samaritans offered to help, how would you have responded? Why did the Jews reject their offer?

_____

_____

_____

2) The Samaritans told the Jews, "We seek your God as you do" (Ezra 4:2). In what ways was this partially true? In what ways was it false? Why did it matter?

_____

_____

_____

3) What tactics did the Samaritans use to discourage the people of Judah? What turned out to be the most effective tactic they used against God's people?

_____

_____

_____

4) How did the Jewish people respond when the Persian governor asked them why they had defied an official decree? How would you have responded if you were in their place?

_____

_____

_____

EXPLORING THE MEANING

One cannot serve God and other "gods" at the same time. The people of Samaria had been taught the truths of God's Word, and they understood (at least outwardly) the proper worship of Yahweh. They even embraced that worship and made sacrifices to God on a regular basis. The problem was that they did not renounce their false gods. They hoped to placate the true God while not repenting of their idolatry. To the casual observer they might have appeared as worshipers of Yahweh, but they did not obey His command to turn away from false gods—and God does not share His glory with any mythical pantheon.

People still make this mistake today. Many have been instructed in the truths of God's Word, and they may even regularly attend a local church—but church attendance will not bring salvation. We must _serve God_ and God alone—not both God and the flesh. Jesus was clear on this when He said, "No one can serve two masters; for either he will hate the one and love the other, or else he will be loyal to the one and despise the other. You cannot serve God and mammon" (Matthew 6:24). (*Mammon* refers to the love of material possessions and comforts, but this is only one of the many forms of idolatry which people engage in today.)

Another trap the devil uses is *syncretism*, where people attempt to comingle elements of many different religions into their own personal brand of worship. This is also very common today, as people attempt to amalgamate many contradictory religious systems into their own notions of "transcendence." Even some who purport to teach God's Word are adulterating it with worldly notions of evolution, psychology, and many other false teachings. But Jesus stated clearly, "I am the way, the truth, and the life. No one comes to the Father except through Me" (John 14:6). There is no other way to salvation than through Jesus Christ, and the Lord will not tolerate any adulteration of His Word.

The devil wears many disguises. The Samaritans approached the leaders of Judah with a friendly offer to help them build the temple. They even pointed out that because they worshiped the same God, they should all be working together toward their common goal. To refuse such kindness would be rude at best—a refusal to get along with others, even a self-righteous hypocrisy—yet that is precisely what God's people did. The Jewish leaders refused to permit the Samaritans to participate in the work that God had given to them.

The Jews' refusal, however, was not due to self-righteousness or rudeness but because they recognized the evil one was behind the offer. The Jews did not judge the Samaritans' hearts but simply compared their behavior with God's revelation and recognized the Samaritans did not worship the Lord the way He had commanded. That was enough to cause Judah to reject their offer, whatever spirit lay behind it. Subsequent events proved the offer was made in a spirit of duplicity. The Samaritans were pretending to be friendly while actually being sinister. Solomon warned of such people when he wrote, "Faithful are the wounds of a friend, but the kisses of an enemy are deceitful" (Proverbs 27:6).

Paul further warned us, "Satan himself transforms himself into an angel of light. Therefore it is no great thing if his ministers also transform themselves into ministers of righteousness, whose end will be according to their works" (2 Corinthians 11:14–15). In other words, Christians must be on guard against those who pretend to be godly but are not, because there are many who try to "transform themselves into ministers of righteousness" by wearing a false disguise. Jesus warned us, "Behold, I send you out as sheep in the midst of wolves. Therefore be wise as serpents and harmless as doves" (Matthew 10:16). Christians should never practice hypocrisy or false pretense, but the devil always does.

God commands us to resist discouragement. The enemies of God's people attempted to interrupt their works of obedience by causing them to become discouraged. The *King James Version* renders Ezra 4:4: "The people of the land weakened the hands of the people of Judah," which captures the essence of discouragement—to become weak, to sink down, to lose the ability to carry on, and to let God's projects drop from despair.

Fear is at the root of discouragement. We are suddenly faced with a circumstance that is beyond our control, and we quickly begin to fear that it is beyond *God's* control as well. And if it is beyond God's control, we might as well just give up now—which is, of course, precisely what Satan is hoping that we will do! However, God commands us to not give in to fear but to strengthen our hands when they become weak (see Isaiah 41:10; Hebrews 12:12).

The best way for us to do this, wrote the author of Hebrews, is to "consider Him who endured such hostility from sinners against Himself, lest you become weary and discouraged in your souls" (12:3). We must remember that Jesus Himself faced immense opposition—more severe than any we will ever face. Yet He overcame it all through the faithfulness of God and through utter confidence in and reliance on God's sovereignty.

REFLECTING ON THE TEXT

5) Why were the Samaritans not qualified to participate in the work of building the temple? What was wrong with their worship of God? Why are such matters important to God?

_____

_____

_____

6) What is the difference between discerning false motives and judging other people? What does it mean to be "wise as serpents and harmless as doves" (Matthew 10:16)? How is this done?

_____

_____

_____

_____

7) How is discouragement related to fear? How is fear related to faith? What is the solution to discouragement? What role do a person's deliberate choices play?

_____

_____

_____

_____

8) What elements of syncretism (blending false religions with God's Word) are being taught today? How can a Christian discern such false teachings?

_____

_____

_____

_____

PERSONAL RESPONSE

9) Is someone or something discouraging you from doing the will of God? How can the example of Jesus give you courage and perseverance? What can other Christians do to help you?

_____

_____

_____

_____

10) Are you trying to serve two masters? What is competing with your loyalty to Christ? What will you do to remove that from your life?

_____

_____

_____

_____

4

CHOOSING GOD'S PRIORITIES
Haggai 1:1–2:9

DRAWING NEAR

What are some comparisons people make when it comes to a home, a car, or success? What traps do people fall into when they compare their situation to the situation of others?

_____

_____

_____

THE CONTEXT

Haggai was a prophet of the Lord in Jerusalem during the time of Zerubbabel. Essentially nothing is known about him apart from his own writings and the mentions made in Ezra, yet he is specific as to the dates of his prophecies: a four-month period during 520 BC. He most likely had returned from Babylon to Jerusalem with Zerubbabel eighteen years earlier, in 538 BC, and he might even have been old enough to have been carried into captivity with Daniel in 586 BC.

The name Haggai means "festival." At first glance this name may seem quite ironic, given the disciplinary content of his message from God. But the

Lord had sent His people to Jerusalem specifically to reinstate His prescribed worship practices and to rebuild His chosen city, which *should* have been a festive occasion. If there was any loss of festivity, it was because the Lord's people had lost His perspective.

As we have seen, the people had become discouraged by the opposition of their neighbors and had wrongly concluded it was not yet time for them to rebuild the temple. So instead, they turned to expanding their own wealth. Like their ancestors who had been exiled before them, they ceased caring about God's kingdom and started building their own. With a biting query, the Lord reminded them it was not right for them to live in paneled houses while the temple lay in ruins. He urged them to consider the consequences of their indifference.

In this study, we will learn that the Lord wants His people to share His priorities, and we will discover what He sometimes does to get our attention. The central message of Haggai is vital to us today: consider your ways!

KEYS TO THE TEXT

Read Haggai 1:1–2:9, noting the key words and phrases indicated below.

MAKING EXCUSES: The Jews in Jerusalem have stopped building the temple, at first by compulsion but now by choice. So the Lord sends His prophet with an important message.

1. THE SECOND YEAR OF KING DARIUS: Not to be confused with Darius the Mede (see Daniel 5:31), Darius I (Hystaspes) became king of Persia in 521 BC, having ascended to the throne after the death of Cambyses. As an officer of Cambyses and the great-grandson of Cyrus the Great's brother, Darius retained the loyalty of the Persian army and thereby defeated other contenders for the throne. He reigned until his death in 486 BC.

IN THE SIXTH MONTH, ON THE FIRST DAY: This first day of the month of Elul in the Jewish calendar would correspond to August 29, 520 BC.

HAGGAI THE PROPHET: Little is known about Haggai apart from what he tells us in this book. He apparently traveled with Zerubbabel in the first wave of Jews returning to Jerusalem.

ZERUBBABEL ... GOVERNOR OF JUDAH: As previously mentioned, Zerubbabel was the grandson of King Jehoiachin and in the Davidic line. Although he is not to be identified with Sheshbazzar (see Ezra 1:8), his role as civil leader and overseer of the temple rebuilding project is certain. He reestablished the Davidic throne, though it would not again be occupied until the time of the Messiah.

JOSHUA ... THE HIGH PRIEST: Spelled *Jeshua* in Ezra 3:2, this man was a descendant of Jehozadak (see 1 Chronicles 6:15) and the religious leader of the exilic community that returned to Jerusalem. He reestablished the high priestly line of Aaron though Eleazar. His father, Jehozadak, had been one of Nebuchadnezzar's captives.

2. THE TIME HAS NOT COME: Haggai began his message by quoting a popular expression of the people who said it was not time to build the temple. Although they had endured the hostile opposition of their neighbors and the lack of economic prosperity, the roots of their reluctance lay ultimately in their selfish indifference to the Lord. Notice also that God referred to the Jews as "this people" rather than "My people." It would be comparable to an angry man referring to his spouse as "this woman" rather than "my wife."

4. TIME FOR YOU YOURSELVES TO DWELL IN YOUR PANELED HOUSES: Walls and ceilings overlaid with cedar were common in wealthy residences. There is a biting irony in the Lord's words. If Jewish exiles' own houses were falling apart, they would not casually say, "The time just hasn't come yet for us to repair the roof." The Lord's people had made their own comfort a high priority while caring nothing about the Lord's house. They were building luxury onto their houses, while the Lord's house was in ruins.

> GET BUSY: *The Lord commands His people to stop making excuses, make His priorities their priorities, and resume the work on rebuilding the temple.*

5. CONSIDER YOUR WAYS: This is the central message of Haggai's prophecies. He called on God's people to take stock of their lives, ensure they were living in obedience to God's Word, and make sure they were sharing His priorities as their own top priorities.

6. YOU HAVE SOWN MUCH, AND BRING IN LITTLE: Ironically, the people had stopped working on the temple to save riches for themselves, yet the Lord was disciplining them by sending drought and famine. The more they saved,

the less they had. However, Haggai says, if they would make God's priorities their own, He would once again send them fullness and prosperity.

8. GO UP . . . AND BRING WOOD AND BUILD: Three relatively simple steps outline what the Lord required of His people in this project. They were to go to the forests (which had regrown during the captivity), make lumber, and start building. By putting God first, they would honor Him in their worship, and they would be blessed in the secondary matters of life. There was no mystery surrounding the Lord's will, and the people did not lack knowledge of what His plan was for them. What they lacked was simple obedience.

THAT I MAY TAKE PLEASURE IN IT: The Lord's pleasure would not come from the building itself. In fact, this temple was to be a pitiful structure compared to the magnificent temple that Solomon had built (see 2 Chronicles 2–5). Rather, the Lord would take pleasure in seeing His chosen people worshiping Him in the way He had prescribed, and His name would be glorified when the world saw them doing so.

9. I BLEW IT AWAY: Literally, "I sniffed at it!" The Lord snorted with contempt when He saw His people's priorities as they strove after the things of this world that would not last.

EVERY ONE OF YOU RUNS TO HIS OWN HOUSE: That is, the Jews were busy running to and fro, looking after their own interests, while the house of the Lord lay in ruins. Jesus addressed this same conflict of priorities when He said, "Do not worry, saying, 'What shall we eat?' or ' What shall we drink?' or 'What shall we wear?' For after all these things the Gentiles seek. For your heavenly Father knows that you need all these things. But seek first the kingdom of God and His righteousness, and all these things shall be added to you" (Matthew 6:31–33).

11. ON ALL THE LABOR OF YOUR HANDS: The price of the people's disobedience had come in the form of an economic catastrophe resulting from God withholding the summer dew. Grain, wine, and oil—the primary crops of the land—could not grow, and the cattle also languished because of the absence of the people's spiritual health. Yet the Lord sent not only drought and famine on the people but also futility and frustration on all their labors. He longed to bless their work with success, but first their work needed to be *His* work.

12. THE PEOPLE FEARED THE PRESENCE OF THE LORD: The exiles who had returned from Persia took Haggai's message to heart. They realized the words of the prophet were from the Lord and "obeyed" and "feared," knowing

that God was present. They renewed their commitment to Him and to seeking His presence. The people's repentance had come less than two weeks after Haggai began prophesying on September 21, 520 BC.

13. I AM WITH YOU: As soon as the people repented of their false priorities and embraced God's priorities once again, the Lord relented His hand of discipline in their lives and began to pour out His blessings. These words are among the most joyful and encouraging words of Scripture. They serve to continually remind us that the almighty God is always with His people in whatever situation they face.

14. STIRRED UP THE SPIRIT: The Lord energized the leaders and the people through His Word to carry on the work of rebuilding the temple. God had sovereignly moved in the heart of Cyrus the Great sixteen years earlier, and now the people's response of repentance and obedience allowed God's Spirit to also energize them for the task.

THE LATTER TEMPLE: *The Lord sends another prophecy through Haggai, this time concerning events in the distant future, when God would build His most glorious temple.*

2:1. IN THE SEVENTH MONTH: This twenty-first day in the Jewish month of Tishri corresponds to October 17, 520 BC. According to Leviticus 23:39–44, this would be the final day of the Feast of Tabernacles, in which the people celebrated God's provision for the Israelites during their forty years of wilderness wanderings and gave thanks for a bountiful harvest. On this occasion, the Lord gave Haggai another message to give to the people.

2. TO THE REMNANT OF THE PEOPLE: Haggai's first message had been directed toward the leaders, Zerubbabel and Joshua. But in this message the prophet includes the remainder of the exiles who returned from Babylon.

3. IS THIS NOT IN YOUR EYES AS NOTHING: The older Jews would have remembered the magnificence and splendor of Solomon's temple, and this rebuilt one must have seemed like a hovel when compared to that structure. Yet the Lord was not discouraged, nor did He want His people to succumb to discouragement. He had a far more glorious temple in the works that no man had ever dreamed of—one not made by human hands.

4. BE STRONG: On the surface, this may sound like a platitude, similar to "cheer up." But the Lord was actually commanding His people to be strong.

Strength is generally something that is not a matter of choice—a person is either physically powerful or not, according to the bodily structure with which he or she was born. Yet the strength the Lord commands *is* a matter of choice: the choice to set one's heart on steadfast obedience regardless of the cost.

5. DO NOT FEAR: Closely related to the previous command is the command not to fear. The Israelites would have been discouraged by the small size of this temple, compared to their previous one, but God did not want them to fear the future because He had a plan that was greater than anything they could imagine. His covenant commitment and the promise that His Spirit would be with them as "when you came out of Egypt" would have been most reassuring.

6. I WILL SHAKE: The shaking of the cosmic bodies and the nations would go beyond the historical removal of kingdoms and the establishment of others, such as the defeat of Persia by Greece (see Daniel 7). Rather, the text looks to the cataclysm in the universe described in Revelation 6–19, the subjugation of the nations by the Messiah, and the setting up of His kingdom that will never be destroyed (see Hebrews 12:25–28; Revelation 6–9).

7. DESIRE OF ALL NATIONS: While some view this phrase as referring to Jerusalem (see Ezra 6:3–9), it seems preferable to view it here as a reference here to the Messiah, the deliverer for whom all the nations ultimately long.

I WILL FILL THIS TEMPLE WITH GLORY: God had filled the first temple built during the days of Solomon with His Shekinah glory, but there no evidence from Scripture that indicates His glory ever did come to Zerubbabel's temple. Nor can this glorification refer to Christ's physical presence in Herod's temple, because the events of verses 6–9 cannot be accounted for historically. The context speaks of the establishment of God's earthly, Davidic, millennial kingdom and His presence in the temple during that kingdom (see Ezekiel 43:5).

8. THE SILVER IS MINE, AND THE GOLD IS MINE: God reassured the people, who were economically destitute, that He was the possessor of all things.

9. THIS LATTER TEMPLE: Haggai's audience might have thought that the temple they were building was "the latter temple," but as we've seen, the Lord's prophecy went far into the future. This temple would vastly surpass any man-made structure in glory, and the nations of the earth would come to it for worship.

I WILL GIVE PEACE: This peace is not limited to the peace that God gives to believers (see Romans 5:1), but looks ahead to that ultimate peace when Christ returns to rule as the Prince of Peace on the throne of David in Jerusalem (see Acts 2:30).

UNLEASHING THE TEXT

1) Why did the Jews stop building the temple in the first place? How did that gradually grow into complacency over time?

_____

_____

_____

2) God does not dwell in any physical structure, so why was He angry the people had not rebuilt His house? What were the larger issues involved?

_____

_____

_____

3) How did the Lord get His message across to His people? What circumstances did He use? What people did He use? How does He do similar things today?

_____

_____

_____

4) What does it mean to be strong? What does it mean to not fear? How are these things done voluntarily?

_____

_____

_____

EXPLORING THE MEANING

It is wise to consider your ways. The Lord sent His prophet Haggai to bring one clear message to His people: obey God even when the circumstances are difficult. The prophet proclaimed, "Consider your ways!" (Haggai 1:5). This command might be translated, "Set your mind on your way of life." In other words, it was a call for the people to consider their ultimate priorities. In effect, God proclaimed, "Make *your* priorities *My* priorities!"

This is an important discipline that God's people need to exercise on a regular basis. The priorities and perspectives of the world are *not* God's views, yet they have a way of seeping into our thinking without our even being aware of it. As Christians, we need to reassess our priorities and views daily, even moment by moment, to ensure that we are thinking the way God thinks. We do this by spending time daily studying and meditating on His Word, by seeking His wisdom through prayer, and by fellowshipping with other believers.

Paul warns his readers that this process is vital if we are to understand God's will for our lives. "I beseech you therefore, brethren, by the mercies of God, that you present your bodies a living sacrifice, holy, acceptable to God, which is your reasonable service. And do not be conformed to this world, but be transformed by the renewing of your mind, that you may prove what is that good and acceptable and perfect will of God" (Romans 12:1–2). Christians cannot hope to understand God's perfect will unless they are constantly renewing their minds by the Word of God. If we forget to consider our ways, we will wind up conformed to this world.

God may use obstacles and setbacks to get your attention. The Jews living in Jerusalem had returned to God's chosen city in order to obey His commands. They had reestablished His prescribed worship practices and started rebuilding the temple and walls. Yet as time went along, they found themselves suffering hardship. They were faced with drought and famine, nothing seemed to prosper, and everything they undertook was met with frustration and failure. Surely this couldn't be God's will for His people who were doing His work!

But that, of course, was exactly the case. The problem was that the people were not doing *God's* work but their *own* work. They were pursuing their own goals, and the Lord needed to send hardship into their lives to get their attention. This is the flip side to a principle we considered previously that Christians should expect opposition when doing the Lord's work. The caveat to that principle is that we should not ignore opposition in case the Lord is using it to get our attention. And, in this study, we see how He sometimes does that.

This principle holds as true for us today as it did for the people in Haggai's day. When God's people refuse to share His priorities and to view the world from His perspective, He will send hardship, frustration, and obstacles intended to make us stop and look up. The great irony is that when the people stopped pursuing God and focused on their own needs, their own needs were not met. The more they put in their own pockets, the less they had for themselves. Likewise, when we turn away from pursuing Christ, we are consumed by the love of the world, which can never satisfy. True satisfaction can only be found in living for Jesus. So we must always consider our ways and renew our godly perspective, for the Lord might send chastening to us in order to keep us from conforming to the world.

There awaits a future glorious kingdom. The Jews of Haggai's day were discouraged. They had returned from exile and labored diligently on the temple. Even when they were distracted from their task and the prophet had to rebuke them, they responded faithfully and resumed the Lord's work. However, with the finished temple now before them, they wept. The temple was small, and the few in the crowd who were old enough to remember Solomon's temple— destroyed seventy years earlier—were dismayed by the comparison. For many of the Israelites, all that was lost in the exile was finally starting to sink in.

The Lord used Haggai to encourage this beleaguered group. He pointed them to the future—to a time when a new temple would stand in Jerusalem. The very spot where they were now weeping would one day be the site of a temple the likes of which the world has never seen. It would be so glorious that the nations of the world would bring their gold and silver to Jerusalem, and the people would worship there (see Haggai 2:6–8). But the glory of this temple, which is also described in Ezekiel 40–48, is not found in the gold and the silver, or even in the people. Rather, Haggai said, from this temple the Lord will give peace to the world.

We find ourselves in a similar place as the Jews in Haggai's day. The gospel has gone forth, and there are Christians around the world. Nevertheless, the world is dominated by wars and rumors of wars. Injustice is the norm, and hunger and poverty are rampant. Yet we, too, can be encouraged by the promise of God that Jesus is going to return to earth and fulfill every one of His promises. We know that He will establish His glorious kingdom on earth, and from that temple God will return peace and order to the world.

REFLECTING ON THE TEXT

5) What exactly is complacency? What causes it and what are its results? How can a Christian guard against it?

_____

_____

_____

6) What does it mean to consider one's ways? How is this done, in practical terms? Why is it so vital for Christians to do?

_____

_____

_____

7) Why do people often lose sight of the Lord's priorities in the midst of their busy lives? How do the demands of daily life crowd out concern about the things of God? How should Christians guard against this?

_____

_____

_____

_____

8) Why were the Jews distressed when they saw their new temple? How did Haggai encourage them? How are Haggai's words encouraging to us today?

_____

_____

_____

PERSONAL RESPONSE

9) Are you facing hardship or obstacles in your life at present? Are they in opposition to the Lord's work or the Lord's attempt to get your attention? Explain.

_____

_____

_____

10) What priorities and perspectives do you share with God? Which priorities or perspectives are more like those of the world? What will you do this week to renew your mind?

_____

_____

_____

5

OBEDIENCE OVER OBSERVANCE
Zechariah 7:1–8:23

DRAWING NEAR

What are some holidays or other observances that today have lost connection to what they were originally intended to celebrate? Why does this happen over time?

_____

_____

_____

_____

THE CONTEXT

Zechariah was a priest who—much like the prophet Haggai—traveled back to Judah with the first wave of exiles under the leadership of Zerubbabel. Tradition holds that he was also a member of the Great Synagogue, a council of 120 men originated by Nehemiah and presided over by Ezra. (This council later developed into the ruling elders of the nation, called the Sanhedrin.) He is occasionally referred to as the son of his grandfather, with whom he traveled to Judah, so it is thought that his father may have died when Zechariah was young.

Zechariah was a contemporary of Haggai and began his ministry two months after Haggai gave his first prophecies. The Lord used Haggai to begin a revival, and He subsequently used Zechariah to keep it going strong. Following the time of Zechariah, the Lord would raise up one final prophet named Malachi to rebuke and condemn the exiles for the abuses they committed during the period of Nehemiah's absence (c. 433–424 BC). After Malachi, prophecy from the Lord would fall silent for 400 years, until a man named John the Baptist arrived on the Judean scene and "came baptizing in the wilderness and preaching a baptism of repentance for the remission of sins" (Mark 1:4).

The Lord used Zechariah during a crucial time in His people's history to bring a rich outburst of promise for the future and sustain the faithful remnant. But first He asked His people to examine their hearts and motives. Fasting and sacrifice have a place, but as should be clear by this point in the study, God is far more interested in something else: *obedience*.

Keys to the Text

Read Zechariah 7:1–8:23, noting the key words and phrases indicated below.

A QUESTION OF RELIGIOUS OBSERVANCE: Now that the temple is being rebuilt, some Jews travel to Jerusalem to seek the Lord's will about whether they should continue their annual fasts.

1. IN THE FOURTH YEAR OF KING DARIUS: Zechariah was living in Jerusalem at the same time as Haggai and had joined Zerubbabel in the first wave of exiles returning to Judah. He gave the prophecies of this chapter in November–December 518 BC, about two years before the temple was completed.

2. TO THE HOUSE OF GOD: While the phrase "house of the LORD" is used of the temple some 250 times in the Old Testament, nowhere else does Bethel (which means "house of God") refer to the temple. The word is thus best viewed as a reference to a city and not the temple. These men came *from* rather than *to* Bethel, a town twelve miles north of Jerusalem. Since the return from Babylon, the Jews had rebuilt and reinhabited that city.

3. SHOULD I WEEP: These men had journeyed from Bethel to Jerusalem to ask the priests whether they needed to continue observing a regular schedule of

fasts. The only fast required by God's Law was the Day of Atonement (see Leviticus 23:27), though God called for other occasional fasts (see Joel 1:12–14). The Jews remembered the fall of Jerusalem by four fasts during the fourth, fifth, seventh, and tenth months. Because the temple had been burned in the fifth month (July–August), that fast was considered the most serious and, thus, the delegation uses it as the test case. They had kept this wailing and fasting for "many years," but now it seemed a wearisome ritual in light of their present prosperity.

> GOD'S FIRST RESPONSE: *In the first of four responses to the question, the Lord asks the people to examine their hearts. What is their real reason for fasting?*

5. SEVENTH MONTHS: This fast mourned the death of Gedaliah, the governor appointed by Nebuchadnezzar (see 2 Kings 25:22–26) after the fall of Jerusalem in 586 BC.

DID YOU REALLY FAST FOR ME: The Lord sent a total of four responses to the question of fasting, with this first one being a rebuke. The Jews, He pointed out, were not actually fasting from repentant sorrow but only out of self-pity (see Isaiah 58:3–9).

6. DO YOU NOT EAT AND DRINK FOR YOURSELVES: The Lord was asking His people to truthfully examine their hearts before Him, laying bare the true motives behind both their fasting and their eating. If their eating was for their own pleasure, the fasts were likely also driven by selfish motivations. If the people had genuinely repented of the idolatry that led them into captivity, they could stop their regimen of fasting, as the temple was now being rebuilt. But if their fasting was not from true repentance, it had been a waste of time.

7. SHOULD YOU NOT HAVE OBEYED: God was stating that if the people of Judah had obeyed His Word in the first place, there would never have been any call for their self-imposed fasts. The important matter was not ritual but obedience. In the past it had been obedience to God's Word that brought great joy, peace, and prosperity to Israel during the time of David and Solomon. If the present generation in Zechariah's time were to substitute ritual for obedience, they would lose the joy, peace, and prosperity they were enjoying. God wanted them to show their repentance through obedience, not through pious religious observances.

THE SOUTH AND THE LOWLAND: A reference to the area south of Beersheba and the Mediterranean coastal plain, encompassing the land from south to west.

GOD'S SECOND RESPONSE: *The Lord now moves to more practical matters in His answer, calling His people to concern themselves with obedience more than with fasting.*

9. EXECUTE TRUE JUSTICE: The Lord here offered some practical examples of the type of obedience He desired. Widows, orphans, and foreigners who lived among the Jews had no advocate to plead their cause and were easy targets for political and financial oppression. God instructed his people to show mercy and compassion to these individuals and to treat them as brothers. For the Lord, true justice was not influenced by a person's wealth or status, nor was it guided by any political agenda. Those who looked for every opportunity to advance themselves would only end up planning evil against others, hoping to maneuver themselves ahead. The Lord said to repent of such things, and they would have no call to be fasting.

11. BUT THEY REFUSED TO HEED: The Lord next pointed out that the Jews' forebears had been told these exact same things—yet they had deliberately and steadfastly refused to listen. The implication of this was a warning to the present generation not to repeat the stubbornness of the previous generation but to yield their hearts and minds in obedience to God's Word. They were to demonstrate their godliness through loving obedience rather than outward displays of piety.

12. THUS GREAT WRATH CAME: The Holy Spirit had served a vital function in the revelation and inspiration of God's Word through human authors, but the people of Judah and Israel had not listened to them. The Lord was gently reminding His people that since He had not spared previous generations from stern discipline for their stubborn sinfulness, He would not spare them either if they refused to listen.

13. I WOULD NOT LISTEN: The previous generation had plugged their ears and hardened their hearts deliberately in order to not hear the Lord's voice, so He responded by doing the same to them. When they cried out for deliverance from captivity, He did not answer.

14. I SCATTERED THEM: This of course refers to the captivity and dispersion of the people, in addition to the desolation of the land in their absence.

GOD'S THIRD RESPONSE: *The Lord now turns His eyes forward to describe a future time of blessing that will extend far beyond the Jews' immediate concerns.*

8:2. THUS SAYS THE LORD OF HOSTS: This is the Lord's third response to the Jews' question concerning their fasting. Zechariah would now contrast Israel's past judgment with the promised future restoration. In light of past captivity, the nation was to repent and live righteously; in light of promised future blessings, Israel was to repent and live righteously.

I AM ZEALOUS FOR ZION WITH GREAT ZEAL: This strong language, emphasizing the Lord's zeal with a triple repetition, expressed the idea that God could not bear the estrangement from His chosen people that had been brought about by their sin. He ached and yearned to be reconciled with them and to reveal His glory among them once again. His love for Israel was so great that He would come in full presence to them again and dwell with His people.

3. I WILL RETURN TO ZION: This promise had many levels. Most immediately, the Lord promised that He would establish His temple once again in Jerusalem. (Zion was the mountain on which ancient Jerusalem was built, which became a name for the city.) But the day would also come when God would enter Zion in the physical form of Jesus Christ. Ultimately, Christ will return to Jerusalem on a future day to establish His thousand-year kingdom on earth.

4–5. OLD MEN AND OLD WOMEN . . . BOYS AND GIRLS: The Lord had commanded His people to look after those who were weak and easily oppressed. However, in the coming day there would be no enemy to threaten any of His people, as the Lord Himself would rule over the whole earth, being physically present in Jerusalem.

6. IF IT IS MARVELOUS IN THE EYES OF THE REMNANT: That is, the Jews of Zechariah's day might have thought these promises sounded marvelous or hard to believe, but their lack of belief and understanding did not limit God in any way. There is nothing too hard for the Lord, and He always keeps His promises—even those that seem far-fetched (see Matthew 1:23).

8. THEY SHALL DWELL IN THE MIDST OF JERUSALEM: The context assures that this return speaks of a worldwide regathering at the Second Advent of Christ. The return from Babylon cannot be in view, as Israel had not been scattered to the west until the diaspora engineered by the Romans during the first century AD.

GOD'S FOURTH RESPONSE: *The Lord continues to expound on the countless blessings He intends for His people. In the end, His answer to their question is simple: obey Me.*

9. LET YOUR HANDS BE STRONG: Here again the Lord commands His people to be resolute in their obedience. Strength of character and faith are signs of devotion to the Lord, and here that devotion was seen specifically in the rebuilding of His temple.

9. BY THE MOUTH OF THE PROPHETS: This refers to Haggai and Zechariah, and there were possibly some other non-writing prophets included as well.

10. BEFORE THESE DAYS: Zechariah recalled the immediate years prior to 520 BC (described in Haggai 1:6–11) when the people's hassles and intrigues with the Samaritans and their love of ease and comfort created an indifference in them toward building the temple. As we have seen, this resulted in divine punishment in the form of great economic distress. However, since the people had again started to build the temple, God would not treat the people as He had those described in this verse.

12. THE SEED SHALL BE PROSPEROUS: These promises of blessing applied in some measure to the Jews of Zechariah's day, but they also pointed to the future day of Christ's millennial kingdom, when God will restore the nation of Israel to full fellowship and reconciliation.

15. DO NOT FEAR: Notice how frequently God gave this command in Zechariah's prophecies. Fear is the enemy of faith and causes a person to doubt that God is in control in the face of overwhelming situations. The Lord was reiterating the important truth of His absolute sovereignty over all events, as well as His unshakable commitment to show forth His blessings and faithfulness to His people. This same truth is vital for Christians of all ages, and we are commanded by God to resist fear through faith in His sovereignty.

16. THESE ARE THE THINGS YOU SHALL DO: As always, the promised blessings were connected with obedience to God's righteous standards. Such obedience can only be brought about by the power of the Spirit in the life of a person who has been transformed by God's grace through faith. These standards are reminiscent of Psalms 15:1–5; 24:4; and Proverbs 6:20–22.

17. ALL THESE ARE THINGS THAT I HATE: As God's people learn to share His priorities, they will grow to hate lies and evil as much as the Lord does.

19. THE FAST OF THE FOURTH MONTH: This was the Lord's fourth and ultimate answer to the Jews' question concerning their self-appointed fasts: turn the fasts into feasts of joy to rejoice over God's blessings and faithfulness. They were to remember, whether in feasting or fasting, to "love truth and peace," for obedience was better than any form of religious observance.

FAST OF THE TENTH: Two other fasts were held in addition to the fasts of the fifth and seventh months (see Zechariah 7:3–5). In the fourth month, the Jews commemorated the breaching of the wall of Jerusalem. In the tenth month, they remembered the beginning of the final siege of Jerusalem, which began in 588 BC.

22. MANY PEOPLES AND STRONG NATIONS: Israel's restoration in millennial glory would be the means of blessing the entire world. Gentiles from around the world would make a pilgrimage to Jerusalem to entreat the Lord. This signifies salvation of people from all over the world during the kingdom, fulfilling the words of Psalm 122.

23. IN THOSE DAYS: In the days in which the messianic kingdom on earth is inaugurated, the Jews will truly be God's messengers as originally intended and will bring multitudes to Christ. The ten-to-one ratio represents a vast number of Gentiles who will come. The Messiah, in the midst of millennial Israel, will be the attraction of the world. When these Gentiles see the Jews being so blessed in their kingdom, they will demand to go to meet the Savior King.

UNLEASHING THE TEXT

1) Why had the Jews observed this cycle of fasting for so many years? What did it represent in their view? What did it represent in God's view?

_____

_____

_____

_____

2) What is the difference between repentance of sin and sorrow over the consequences? How does a Christian distinguish between them? What is the outward result of each?

_____

_____

_____

3) Define the following in your own words, giving practical examples of each.

Mercy:

_____

_____

_____

Compassion:

_____

_____

_____

Oppression of widows or the fatherless:

_____

_____

_____

Oppression of foreigners or the poor:

_____

_____

_____

Planning evil in your heart:

_____

_____

_____

4) In what sense are religious observances a waste of time? When are they valuable? How can a Christian distinguish between these two situations?

_____

_____

_____

_____

EXPLORING THE MEANING

Obedience is better than sacrifice and fasting. The Jews traveled to Jerusalem to seek the Lord's guidance concerning an annual series of fasts they had observed since the beginning of their captivity seventy years earlier. The fasts brought a degree of hardship on the people, as they involved times of mourning and self-denial as well as abstinence from food. The fasts were intended to represent the people's mourning over the Lord's judgment when He permitted the Babylonians to destroy Jerusalem, but now that the city was being rebuilt and temple worship was being reestablished, they wondered if God would object if they ended these observances.

As we have seen, the Lord was more concerned about the people's obedience than with their outward displays of religion. It is true that the Jews demonstrated a desire to obey by asking the Lord's guidance on the matter, but God probed deeper into their hearts, asking them where their deepest priorities lay. Were they truly committed to obeying His Word, or were they mostly concerned with their own comfort? Would they serve Him with whole hearts, as their predecessor David did? Or would they be only halfhearted, like Solomon, and eventually wander back to foreign gods? Were they more concerned with obedience to God or with outward demonstrations of religious regulations?

The Lord had addressed these questions in more detail through His prophet Isaiah. The people, He said, had performed fasts and acts of penitence on the outside, while their hearts were still wicked on the inside. The Lord wanted full obedience to His Word, not mere showmanship during occasional religious observances. "Is this not the fast that I have chosen," the Lord asked, "to loose the bonds of wickedness, to undo the heavy burdens, to let the oppressed go free, and that you break every yoke?" (Isaiah 58:6). Samuel gave Saul similar counsel: "Has the LORD as great delight in burnt offerings and sacrifices, as in obeying the voice of the LORD? Behold, to obey is better than sacrifice, and to heed than the fat of rams" (1 Samuel 15:22). Obedience to God's Word is the only sacrifice the Lord wants from His people.

The Lord yearns for our fellowship. The Lord told His people, "I am zealous for Zion with great zeal; with great fervor I am zealous for her" (Zechariah 8:2). Many modern Bibles translate "fervor" as "wrath," which captures the burning passion the Lord was expressing. "I burn for you with a jealous fire," the Lord was effectively saying, "a zealous and jealous love that will tolerate no competition." The Lord yearned so deeply for the fellowship of His people that it was like a consuming fire, destroying anything that prevented their full reconciliation.

It is interesting that the Lord referred to the zeal of His love in this context. The Jews had been zealous themselves in maintaining a cycle of fasts over a period of seventy years during their captivity. "Should I weep in the fifth month and fast as I have done for so many years?" they asked (Zechariah 7:3). Their question implied that they had not permitted anything to prevent them from keeping this religious observance, but the Lord called them to search their hearts and question why they were truly fasting. Were they mourning the loss of God's close fellowship, which they had once enjoyed as His chosen nation? Or were they mourning over their own suffering and misfortune? The two were not the same!

The Lord wanted His people to be zealous in seeking His face and entering His holy presence. Now, this might well be associated with certain spiritual activities, such as commemorating the Lord's Supper as Jesus commanded (see Luke 22), but those activities themselves are hollow and meaningless if one's heart is not fully committed to living in fellowship with God. The Lord has a burning zeal for our fellowship, for our company, and He wants us to have that same zeal for Him.

Jesus is coming again, and the day may be very soon. The Lord's prophecies of blessing in Zechariah 7–8 had some immediate application to the Jews of Zechariah's day, but they also looked forward to future events. For example, His promise to return to Zion (8:3) indicated that He would rebuild His temple in Jerusalem during their day, yet it also looked ahead to the wonderful day when He would enter Jerusalem in physical form through His Son, Jesus Christ. And the promise has yet another level of fulfillment still to come, when Jesus returns to earth to establish His thousand-year earthly kingdom centered in Zion.

The Bible is clear that Jesus is coming again—but this time not as a helpless babe lying in a manger. He will return in His strength and glory, and He will establish a kingdom that rules all the nations of the earth with a "rod of iron" (Psalm 2:9; Revelation 2:27; 19:15). In that day, the nation of Israel shall once again be the seat of blessing to all peoples (see Zechariah 8:13), while the enemies of God and of His people shall be broken without remedy.

We live in the age of grace, when God's gift of salvation is readily available to anyone through faith in the gospel. But the day is coming when the Lord "will gather out of His kingdom all things that offend, and those who practice lawlessness, and will cast them into the furnace of fire. There will be wailing and gnashing of teeth" (Matthew 13:41–42). The day of Christ's return is drawing close. For the Christian, this means to "look up and lift up your heads, because your redemption draws near" (Luke 21:28). But for those who have not received salvation and eternal life through Jesus Christ, the Lord calls out, "Behold, now is the accepted time; behold, now is the day of salvation" (2 Corinthians 6:2).

REFLECTING ON THE TEXT

5) What things does God hate? Why does He hate them? How does your own list of "hates" compare with God's list?

_____

_____

_____

_____

6) The Jews asked a fairly straightforward question, but the Lord's answer was lengthy and complex. What deeper truth was He trying to dig out?

_____

_____

_____

_____

7) What did God mean when He said, "I was zealous for Zion with great zeal; with great fervor I am zealous for her" (Zechariah 8:2)? How does God's zeal for your fellowship compare with yours for His?

_____

_____

_____

_____

8) What are some signs that Jesus' return is imminent? How does this affect your daily life? How might your priorities change in the coming week if you took this to heart?

_____

_____

_____

PERSONAL RESPONSE

9) Does your daily life reflect true obedience to God's Word, or do you tend to "go through the motions" of religious observances? What area of obedience might the Lord be calling you to this week?

_____

_____

_____

10 Have you received God's gift of salvation through Jesus Christ? If not, what is preventing you from doing so right now?

_____

_____

_____

6

The Second Wave of Exiles

Ezra 7:1–8:36

Drawing Near

What are some "shortcuts" that people take when it comes to following the rules? Why is it often so hard for people to obey the letter of the law?

_____

_____

_____

The Context

Ezra was descended from a long line of priests that dated all the way back to Aaron himself, who was the first high priest of Israel (see Exodus 28:1). The Lord had appointed Aaron, Moses' brother, to take on that sacred role, and He had stipulated that only men descended from Aaron should ever follow in his steps. In this alone, Ezra would have been a good choice to lead the Jews back to Jerusalem, as it would have indicated that the people were reestablishing the Lord's prescribed worship in the temple.

However, that was not Ezra's sole qualification as a leader. He also had spent his life studying God's Word and memorizing it—and, more important, he had spent his life *obeying* it. He had become an expert in the law of God, a teacher of teachers, and a teacher by example as well as by word. The Lord had appointed him to take the lead on this important expedition because he was well qualified in obedience as well as knowledge.

In previous studies, we saw how many of the Jews had returned to Jerusalem during the "first wave" of exiles under the leadership of Zerubbabel (c. 538 BC). Now, Ezra himself would gather together the next wave to return to the people's homeland (c. 458 BC). As before, the trip would be long and fraught with danger, but the king had issued a decree giving his blessing, and he had loaded the people with gold and silver to fund the work. Everything was lined up and ready to go—but then Ezra discovered that some people were missing!

In this study, we will look more closely at the life of Ezra and see what made him a godly leader. We will also discover what it means to be a follower of God who does not cut corners.

KEYS TO THE TEXT

Read Ezra 7:1–8:36, noting the key words and phrases indicated below.

THE LORD CALLS EZRA: Ezra is a priest, a scribe, and an expert in the Word of God. The Lord calls him to move to Jerusalem, and he obeys God's command.

1. AFTER THESE THINGS: Zerubbabel led the Jews in rebuilding the temple in Jerusalem, which was finally completed in 515 BC during the reign of King Darius of Persia. The events in Ezra 7 take place many years later, under the reign of King Artaxerxes, when Ezra led a second wave of Jews back to Jerusalem. During the sixty-year interval between Zerubbabel and Ezra, the events of the book of Esther took place in Persia.

6. A SKILLED SCRIBE IN THE LAW OF MOSES: Ezra was descended from a long line of priests, which he traced back all the way to Aaron, the brother of Moses. He was also a scribe, one who studied and transcribed the Law of Moses. This dual role made him a valuable asset to the returning Jews, who were in desperate need of instruction concerning God's Word. Tradition claims that Ezra could write out the entire law from memory.

ACCORDING TO THE HAND OF THE LORD HIS GOD UPON HIM: Once again, we are reminded that all the events in the book of Ezra took place according to the sovereign will of God. Without God's constant intervention and protection, Jerusalem could never have been rebuilt—and for that matter, the Jews themselves would have remained in exile.

7. THE PRIESTS, THE LEVITES . . . AND THE NETHINIM: The priests were descendants of Aaron who served as the nation's spiritual leaders and oversaw the worship and sacrifices. The Levites were members of the priestly tribe of Levi who assisted the priests. The Nethinim were not members of the priestly class but were descendants of the Gibeonites. They were responsible for looking after the temple building. "Joshua made them woodcutters and water carriers for the congregation and for the altar of the LORD" (Joshua 9:27).

8. EZRA CAME TO JERUSALEM: The second wave of exiles' four-month journey from Babylon to Jerusalem, covering almost 1,000 miles, started in March–April and ended in July–August.

10. SEEK . . . DO . . . TEACH: Ezra set an example of the process by which a person grows to spiritual maturity and godliness. First, he "prepared his heart" in a fixed determination to understand the Word of God, probably by spending his youth in the study and meditation of the Scriptures. This process naturally fit together with immediate application, as Ezra strove to do what God's Word commanded, putting it into practice in his own life first. This, finally, led to a natural role as a teacher of others—for one cannot teach what he has not first practiced. Ezra's life of obedience enabled him to teach God's Word; but more important, "the good hand of his God upon him" (verse 9) strengthened and equipped him for that role.

11. COPY OF THE LETTER: The original was usually kept as an official record. This particular letter was addressed to Ezra because the decree recorded therein was the critical administrative document. In essence, it authorized the document into Ezra's hands so he could carry it and read it to its intended audience.

EZRA THE PRIEST, THE SCRIBE, EXPERT: This is a powerful testimony to both Ezra's character and his grasp of God's Word. He had studied and memorized the Lord's commands to the point that he had become a teacher of teachers. It is also significant that he used these roles as his description, rather than "envoy of the king" or some other title.

THE KING'S DECREE: King Artaxerxes writes a decree giving the Jews permission to return to Jerusalem and rebuild God's temple.

12. ARTAXERXES, KING OF KINGS: It was true that Artaxerxes ruled over other kings, but Jesus Christ is the true King of kings and Lord of lords (see Revelation 19:16). Jesus alone can make that claim, for He will rule over all earthly powers in His coming kingdom (see 11:15).

13. I ISSUE A DECREE: Decrees were commonly written as official documents and then reiterated in personal letters that gave an emissary authority in his travels. Ezra would have read this letter to the Jews in Jerusalem to demonstrate that he had the king's backing. This is a remarkable decree that evidences God's sovereign rule over earthly kings and His intent to keep the Abrahamic, Davidic, and New Covenants with Israel.

14. SEVEN COUNSELORS: This number was according to the Persian tradition.

15. FREELY OFFERED TO THE GOD OF ISRAEL: It is interesting that King Artaxerxes chose to make a freewill offering to the Lord, even though he did not worship Him. The king may have been hoping to appease "the God of Judah" in hopes of avoiding future trouble from that region, as the people during that time thought that various gods ruled in specific geographical regions. The fact that Ezra was carrying a bounty of the king's gold and silver would make his journey to Judah that much more dangerous.

16. THE FREEWILL OFFERING OF THE PEOPLE AND THE PRIESTS: The freewill gifts of God's people were an important part of the rebuilding effort in Jerusalem, both for the temple and the walls.

17. NOW THEREFORE: The royal decree protocol recorded in the opening words of verses 13 to 16 lead up to the section introduced by these words.

21. THE GOD OF HEAVEN: The king's use of this phrase suggests that he had some insight into the true nature and character of God, but his repeated references to "your God" and "the God of Jerusalem" indicate that he had probably not bowed himself before the true God of all creation. Knowing who God is does not make a person a Christian—one must also submit to Him as the only God and accept His free gift of salvation. The king's question, "Why should there be wrath against the realm of the king and his sons?" (verse 23), suggests that he viewed the Lord as yet another "god" whose power was limited geographically. Again, his gifts probably were motivated by the hope of appeasing this unknown god of the Jews.

22. ONE HUNDRED TALENTS: This represents nearly four tons in weight; "one hundred kors" is approximately 750 bushels; and "one hundred baths" is 600 gallons.

25. SET MAGISTRATES AND JUDGES . . . AND TEACH: The king had turned to Ezra in a demonstration of administrative trust and granted him permission to appoint magistrates and judges for the region. The effect of this decree gave a measure of autonomy to the Jews in Judah—exactly what their enemies were striving to avoid. Yet this element of spiritual shepherding was exactly what Ezra had a heart to do. He knew the Jews returning from captivity needed instruction in the Word of God, and this became the focus of his ministry.

27. WHO HAS PUT SUCH A THING AS THIS IN THE KING'S HEART: Once again, Ezra recognized the king's generosity was due to the Lord's intervention. He was grateful to King Artaxerxes for his benevolence, but he gave the final glory to God.

PREPARING FOR THE JOURNEY: Ezra gathers together the necessary people and supplies, and they prepare to make the dangerous and lengthy trip to Judah.

8:1. WENT UP WITH ME FROM BABYLON: The list that follows no doubt included those who lived in the surrounding areas. The total number of males in this section was 1,496 plus the men named, so with the addition of the women and children, the number easily approached 7,000 to 8,000. Just as with the first group of returnees, many Jews remained behind in Babylon after this group had departed, content with their established and comfortable lifestyle.

15. THAT FLOWS TO AHAVA: An unknown location where a canal or river flowed into the Euphrates River. This was in Babylon, and Ezra chose it as the place where the returning Jews would render vows for several days in preparation to leave.

THE SONS OF LEVI: That is, men from the tribe of Levi. This tribe had been set apart by God to be the priestly class, and all who acted in a priestly role were descendants of Levi. The high priest was always a descendant of Aaron, a subset of the tribe of Levi, but other Levites also served in other priestly functions. Apparently, no descendant of Levi had joined Ezra for this return to Jerusalem, though others had returned previously with Zerubbabel. Ezra was deeply concerned about this situation, because he had no one qualified to serve in the temple.

17. THEY SHOULD BRING US SERVANTS FOR THE HOUSE OF OUR GOD: To remedy this situation, Ezra took the time and effort to find qualified men from the tribe of Levi. Others might have been tempted to look for some more expedient method—perhaps not being too concerned about meeting the Lord's qualifications for the priestly class—but Ezra was determined to obey the Lord's Word in all things. He especially wanted to obey God's Law in something as important as selecting the nation's spiritual leaders.

18. THEY BROUGHT US A MAN OF UNDERSTANDING: Only thirty-eight Levites were willing to join Ezra in this second return to Jerusalem. However, this remnant of men whom the Lord had raised up had understanding and wisdom and recognized that even the mundane tasks in God's service were of infinitely more value than the most glorified projects of the world. This also helps us recognize the sacrifice that Ezra and Nehemiah paid in leaving behind their great Persian positions to undertake the arduous task of rebuilding Jerusalem.

FINAL PREPARATIONS: *Before Ezra leads the exiles back to Jerusalem, he holds a fast to pray for God's protection and appoints priests to carry the gifts for the temple.*

21. I PROCLAIMED A FAST: The Jews' four-month trek back to Judah would be fraught with dangers, because thieves who robbed people for survival frequented the roads. Even messengers traveled with caravans to ensure their personal safety. However, Ezra and the people did not want to confuse the king about their trust in God's protection, so they entreated the Lord for safety with a prayerful fast. They also wanted their hearts and lives to be pure before Him. God honored their prayer of faith with His protection.

22. AN ESCORT OF SOLDIERS AND HORSEMEN: The presence of the great gift of King Artaxerxes' gold and silver only made the caravan a more attractive target for bandits and enemies. Yet Ezra was "ashamed to request" an escort from the king because he had previously told the Persian monarch that the Lord would protect the Jewish people. He was concerned about the Lord's glory, not about their safety, and he did not want the Persians to think that his God could not live up to His promises. Later, Nehemiah *would* accept his king's offer of a military escort due to the same concerns for his safety.

26. I WEIGHED INTO THEIR HAND: Once again, Ezra carefully followed the Word of God as he gave the sacred treasure into the hands of the priests (see Leviticus 3).

28. YOU ARE HOLY TO THE LORD: The Lord had set apart the tribe of Levi to be His holy priesthood, and as such they were consecrated to His service. He had said to Moses, "Take the Levites instead of all the firstborn among the children of Israel, and the livestock of the Levites instead of their livestock. The Levites shall be Mine" (Numbers 3:45). In the same way, the gold, silver, and other precious objects had been set aside for the Lord's use, and in that sense they were holy in His sight.

31. THE HAND OF OUR GOD WAS UPON US: Once again, Ezra reminded his readers that the Lord is completely faithful to His promises and His people. The Jews had no need of a military escort in spite of the fact that they were carrying a king's ransom in the caravan. The important fact for Christians to understand is that the Lord's hand is always on His children, and He must be the sole source of our security.

31. TWELFTH DAY OF THE FIRST MONTH: The twelve-day delay occurred because of the three-day delay searching for more Levites and the fast.

36. THEY DELIVERED THE KING'S ORDERS: The plural of the word *orders* may account for the change in terminology. This would include the decrees plus other orders in the official correspondence that Artaxerxes gave to Ezra to deliver to support the Jews and their building of the temple.

UNLEASHING THE TEXT

1) According to Ezra 7:10, what three things characterized Ezra's life? How are these things done? Why are they important?

_____

_____

_____

_____

2) How had Ezra become an expert in the Word of God? What effect did that expertise have on his ministry? What impact did it have on the people around him?

_____

_____

_____

3) Why did Ezra feel ashamed to ask the king for a military escort? What motivated his decision? What does this reveal about his character?

_____

_____

_____

4) Why did Ezra take time to find some members of the tribe of Levi before leaving for Jerusalem? What did this demonstrate about God's Word? What did it demonstrate about his level of obedience to God's Law?

_____

_____

_____

_____

EXPLORING THE MEANING

There are no shortcuts in obedience to God's Word. Ezra made many preparations for the move to Jerusalem. He gathered a large body of Jews to join him, and each of those families made all the necessary preparations involved in making a life-changing move. The king had given Ezra his full blessing on the trip and provided him with a letter of authority to reestablish a Jewish community and rebuild the Lord's temple. The king had also handed Ezra a huge sum of money and treasure, and Ezra probably felt a sense of urgency to get that money where it belonged. A host of people and plans were ready to go. But then Ezra made the startling discovery that there were no members of the tribe of Levi with him on the journey.

Human wisdom would suggest a "work-around" measure at this point. So many people were standing around, waiting to get started, and the king's money was just sitting there waiting for theft. Surely, under such circumstances, prudence would dictate an "ad hoc" alternate plan. But Ezra refused to begin rebuilding the temple without the leadership and assistance of God's selected priests because God's Word commanded it. Ezra may have been caught by surprise, but he knew that the Lord was not. God wanted him to follow His prescribed methods, and He would take care of the timetable.

There are no shortcuts to obeying God's Word. The Lord does not call His people to find "work-arounds" or "emergency interim methods." His Word gives clear guidance in our daily lives, the correct approach to worship and church structure, roles of authority and submission, and much more that often goes contrary to what the world believes today. When it comes to the clear teachings in Scripture, there is no substitute for obedience.

The Lord calls us to seek His guidance in every undertaking. Ezra and the Jews were ready to move forward on their expedition back to Jerusalem. They had spent months preparing for the long journey and made arrangements for a permanent change of address. This was no small undertaking. It represented a complete change of lifestyle for everyone concerned, and it is unlikely that anyone had made the decision on the spur of the moment. Yet when the big day had nearly arrived, Ezra stopped everything and called the people to join him in fasting and prayer to seek the Lord's guidance and blessing.

This might seem like an odd approach. After all, this was no last-minute realization that they had forgotten to seek the Lord's guidance. The people in general, and Ezra in particular, had undoubtedly been in *much* prayer during the months of preparation. Nevertheless, when everything was prepared and the people were ready to begin, Ezra once again spent time before the Lord. Ezra had made it a habit of his life to bathe every undertaking in prayer. He constantly sought the Lord's guidance to ensure that he was going in the right direction and not overlooking anything important.

This is the pattern for all God's people, for we are to keep entering His presence deliberately and without distraction. Ezra added the element of fasting in order to dedicate the prayer time fully to the Lord, blocking out all the distractions of daily life to concentrate on His voice. The person who seeks the Lord's direction for every step will never go far from His chosen path.

Study, obey, and teach. In Ezra 7:10 we read, "Ezra had prepared his heart to seek the Law of the LORD, and to do it, and to teach statutes and ordinances in Israel." This statement reveals a great deal about the character of the man: he had "prepared his heart," meaning that he had consciously made it a high priority in his life, and he had stuck to that priority for many years. He had sought the Lord by studying His Word, meditating on it daily, and looking for ways to apply it practically in his life. He probably had also taken great pains to memorize it, as history claims that he could write the Law of Moses from memory. However, beyond even these intellectual pursuits, Ezra had consciously applied God's Word to his life, deliberately obeying His commands on a daily basis for a long period of time.

These habits are what equipped Ezra to become a great teacher. A person cannot hope to teach others how to play a musical instrument until he or she has gained some degree of mastery of that same instrument. In the same way, a person cannot teach others the Word of God unless he or she is already living by it. Not every Christian is a gifted teacher, and not all Christians are called to preach the Word from the pulpit, but every Christian *is* called to teach by example. In fact, some of the most powerful teaching is done simply by living according to God's Word, whether or not any words of explanation are ever given to those watching.

The psalmist summarized this process nicely: "How can a young man cleanse his way? By taking heed according to Your word. With my whole heart I have sought You; oh, let me not wander from Your commandments! Your word I have hidden in my heart, that I might not sin against You" (Psalm 119:9–11). The process illustrated by Ezra is threefold: study God's Word, obey God's Word, and teach God's Word. This is the process all Christians are called to emulate.

REFLECTING ON THE TEXT

5) If you had been in Ezra's place, what would you have done on discovering that you had no priests with you? How would your response have been similar to or different from Ezra's?

_____

_____

_____

_____

6) What shortcuts do some Christians take when it comes to God's Word? What is the danger of such an approach? What shortcuts have you taken in the past?

_____

_____

_____

_____

7) Why did the people take time to fast and pray before leaving on their long journey? Why are the "little ones" mentioned in this context (see 8:21)? What effect would this action of praying and fasting have on their children?

_____

_____

_____

_____

8) Why is it so important for a Christian to spend time alone studying God's Word? What role does fasting play in this process?

_____

_____

_____

PERSONAL RESPONSE

9) What are you teaching to people around you each day concerning God's Word and His character? What might a casual observer learn from watching your life?

_____

_____

_____

10) What decisions are you facing at present? In what ways are you submitting to God's will and casting your worries on Him? How can you do that more this week?

_____

_____

_____

7

UNEQUALLY YOKED
Ezra 9:1–10:44

DRAWING NEAR

How does our culture tend to view marriage between people? How do you think these views are similar to or different from what God thinks about marriage?

_____

_____

_____

THE CONTEXT

We now return to Ezra and his fellow Jews as they embark on their journey to Jerusalem. Ezra reports, "The hand of our God was upon us, and He delivered us from the hand of the enemy and from ambush along the road. So we came to Jerusalem" (8:31–32). Ezra immediately set to work to put everything in order: disseminating the money and treasure the king had given him, appointing spiritual leaders, guiding the people in worship to the Lord, and all the other myriad details involved in establishing a new home for himself and others.

Within four months or so, Ezra was able to complete all of these tasks. It seemed the time was right for him to now "buckle down" and get busy with the project of rebuilding the temple. But no sooner had Ezra gotten things in order than he was confronted with an unexpected problem: many of the Jews had married foreign spouses! This must have seemed incomprehensible to Ezra, since that was the very sin that had led the nation of Israel into captivity in the first place.

However, as we have seen, human nature is always prone to wander from the will of God. Solomon wrote, "As a dog returns to his own vomit, so a fool repeats his folly" (Proverbs 26:11). In this lesson, we will see that while the Jews may have gotten a new start, they were still in need of the new covenant and the Messiah to change their hearts. We will also look at marriage from God's perspective and discover that He takes it very seriously.

KEYS TO THE TEXT

Read Ezra 9:1–10:44, noting the key words and phrases indicated below.

RETURNING TO FORMER SINS: Ezra has just arrived in Jerusalem with a group of returning exiles, and almost immediately the people fall into old patterns of sin.

1. WHEN THESE THINGS WERE DONE: "These things" refers to the implementation of the different trusts and duties that the king had commissioned Ezra to complete. The Jewish people had not been in the land for long when the following events transpired.

THE PRIESTS AND THE LEVITES: As was the case during the Assyrian deportation of Israel and the Babylonian deportation of Judah, the spiritual leadership defaulted along with the people.

HAVE NOT SEPARATED THEMSELVES: The Lord had commanded His people to keep themselves apart from the people of Canaan when they arrived in the Promised Land. In fact, He had even ordered them to make war against many of the pagan nations, destroying their altars and religious sites dedicated to false gods. If the people failed to do this, the Lord warned, they would wind up becoming just like their pagan neighbors—intermarrying and adopting their idolatrous ways (see Exodus 34:10–16; Deuteronomy 7:1–6). Unfortunately, the Israelites did not obey the Lord's commands in this regard, and the Lord sent them into captivity. It was a sad statement on the human condition to find the returning Jews immediately beginning to repeat their former sins. It is compounded by the fact that the priests and Levites—the nation's spiritual leaders—had joined in.

2. **TAKEN SOME OF THEIR DAUGHTERS AS WIVES FOR THEMSELVES:** Malachi added that some of these people had even divorced their Jewish wives in order to marry foreigners (see Malachi 2:11, 14–16).

THE HOLY SEED IS MIXED WITH THE PEOPLES OF THOSE LANDS: This is a powerful expression that can help us understand why God does not want His people to intermarry with unbelievers. The Lord had chosen Abraham and his descendants to be the race into which He would bring Jesus, the Messiah, His holy and sinless Son. As such, the Lord wanted Abraham's descendants to be set apart as a holy people, distinct from the world around them, rather than blending in. This same principle applies to God's people today, for the Christian church is the bride of Christ. The Lord still demands that His bride keep herself apart from the world.

THE HAND OF THE LEADERS AND RULERS HAS BEEN FOREMOST: Once again, it was bad enough that the people of Judah had fallen immediately back into their former sins, but it was unconscionable and inexcusable that the spiritual leaders were actually leading the way. When the leaders go in the wrong direction, the rest of the people can only be expected to follow.

EZRA GRIEVES: Ezra's immediate response is to fall before the Lord in deep mourning. Yet, as God's chosen leader, he identifies himself with the people of God.

3. **I TORE MY GARMENT AND MY ROBE:** Ezra's response was a threefold display of the tremendous grief he felt when he learned of the people's sin. He knew that their wanton disregard of God's Word would lead to sorrow at both the personal and national levels—for the sin that brought God's discipline in the past could only bring it again in the future.

4. **EVERYONE WHO TREMBLED:** There were still some in Judah, including Ezra, who took the Lord's Word seriously. They sat with Ezra until the gathering of the people for the evening sacrifice, during which there was surely public prayer and confession as Ezra fasted, lamented, and prayed in an effort to lead the leaders and people to repent. Their action of gathering with Ezra also made a public statement that they were not joining together with those who were in sin. If God's people refuse to separate themselves from the world, then those who still fear God's Word will separate themselves from them.

6. OUR INIQUITIES . . . OUR HEADS . . . OUR GUILT: Notice how Ezra identified himself with the people who were in sin, even though he had not participated in that sin. He recognized that sin is like leaven: a little bit of it can infect the entire nation. But he was also demonstrating an important element of spiritual leadership by identifying himself with the entire body of God's people and remembering that he, too, was a sinner.

7. WE HAVE BEEN VERY GUILTY: Ezra also understood that God takes sin seriously, and that included the sin of intermarriage and divorce.

8. A PEG IN HIS HOLY PLACE: That is, the remnant of God's people in Judah had been firmly fixed in God's holy place as a peg is firmly fixed in a wall.

9. TO GIVE US A WALL: The Jews as a people group had been scattered all over the Fertile Crescent and were vulnerable to the nations. However, in Judah, with God as protector, they would be safe. The *wall* did not exclude the walls of Jerusalem yet to be built, but it speaks more broadly of God's provision for protection.

10. WE HAVE FORSAKEN YOUR COMMANDMENTS: This was not a quotation from Ezra of any single text of Scripture but rather a summation of God's commands on the subject.

14. NO REMNANT OR SURVIVOR: Ezra feared that this sin would provoke the ultimate judgment of God and the abrogation of the Lord's unconditional covenants. However, while God judges sin, the coming of the Messiah and Paul's insights on God's continued faithfulness in His promise to the Jews assures us that God's calling of Israel as a beloved people and nation is irrevocable (see Romans 11:25–29).

15. NO ONE CAN STAND BEFORE YOU: All the people were reckoned guilty and had no right to stand in God's presence, yet they would penitently seek the grace of forgiveness.

PUTTING AWAY THE WIVES: Ezra's solution to the problem is to call on the people to put away any unbelieving spouses. It is imperative that God's people be separate from the world.

10:1. THE PEOPLE WEPT VERY BITTERLY: When confronted with their sin, the people of Judah did the right thing: they repented and mourned over their wickedness. This is what God desires to see when His people commit sin.

2. SHECHANIAH THE SON OF JEHIEL: This leader, who was not involved in the mixed marriages, was bold and chose to obey God rather than please his relatives.

3. TO PUT AWAY ALL THESE WIVES: Shechaniah called for the people and leaders to accomplish the specific action of divorcing their wives and children and acknowledged that Ezra has counseled a course of action consistent with Scripture (see 2 Chronicles 29:10). We must remember, however, that Ezra is a book of history and records actual historical events. The fact that a person did something in Israel's history does not mean it is a model of God's ideal plan for us to follow, for God hates divorce (see Malachi 2:16).

4. YOUR RESPONSIBILITY: Here again, Shechaniah acknowledged that Ezra was the chief spiritual leader and had appropriate divine authority and the responsibility to take on the execution of this formidable task of dealing with divorces for so many.

6. HE ATE NO BREAD AND DRANK NO WATER: This was an unusually stringent fast, for people generally only fasted from food but not from water. It indicated the depth of Ezra's grief and consternation over this situation, which underscores the seriousness of marrying an unbeliever.

7. THEY ISSUED A PROCLAMATION: A proclamation was delivered orally by a herald and often had the force of law, as did this particular proclamation. Not participating in the assembly, as some might have been tempted to do, meant not just losing your property but also being ostracized from Israel.

8. HE HIMSELF WOULD BE SEPARATED FROM THE ASSEMBLY: The people of Judah needed to separate themselves from anyone who had married an unbeliever, lest the unbeliever in their midst would lead others into idolatry. The people were required to respond within seventy-two hours. Given that only the territories of Judah and Benjamin were involved, the greatest distance for the proclamation to travel would have been no more than forty to fifty miles.

THE PLAN PUT INTO EFFECT: The leaders of Judah agree to Ezra's plan, but they have an issue with how it will be carried out. So they suggest a way to make it more feasible.

13. THERE ARE MANY PEOPLE: This statement demonstrates how widespread the sin was among the people. Due to the large number of people to be processed (in addition to the heavy rains), the whole operation could go on for a long time. So the people made an administrative suggestion for dealing with the magnitude of the problem: for each unlawful marriage, a questioning or court session could be conducted locally.

15. JONATHAN . . . AND JAHAZIAH . . . OPPOSED THIS: It is unclear whether these two, along with Meshullam and Shabbethai, opposed the delay in dealing with the situation or opposed dealing with the sin at all. It was, however, a good plan and brought about a reasonably fast resolution. It took three months for the people to rectify the situation in all cases, after which they were prepared to celebrate Passover.

17. THEY FINISHED QUESTIONING ALL THE MEN: This verse indicates that Ezra and the other spiritual leaders considered each case individually, and it is likely that each foreign wife was given an opportunity to openly forsake her false gods and embrace the only true God. Such repentance would change the marriage from an unequal yoking to a proper marriage between believers. The list of those who divorced their pagan wives seems rather short, considering the frequent references to "many of us" (see verse 13), so it is possible that at least some of the unbelieving spouses repented of their pagan ways and embraced God's truth.

18. THE SONS OF JESHUA THE SON OF JOZADAK: At the head of the list of those who had intermarried were the descendants and other relatives of the high priest who first returned with Zerubbabel and led in the temple reconstruction. They set the example for all the people in giving the appropriate trespass offering (see verse 19).

20. ALSO OF THE SONS OF: Given the fact it took three months to resolve the situation, this list of 113 men could represent only those in leadership. There were apparently more violators among the people, and even though Ezra and the Jewish leaders dealt with the problem directly, it would eventually reappear (see Nehemiah 9–10).

44. BY WHOM THEY HAD CHILDREN: An appropriate provision was doubtlessly made for the divorced wives and the children.

UNLEASHING THE TEXT

1) Why did Ezra respond so vehemently to the Jews' marrying foreigners? Why was that such a big problem for God's people?

_____

_____

_____

2) Why had the Jews married foreigners in the first place? Considering that they had just recently moved to a new home far from Persia, what factors might have made such marriages seem acceptable to them at the time?

_____

_____

_____

3) Why does God condemn marriage between a believing and an unbelieving spouse? What dangers does it pose to the believer? To the children? To the church as a whole?

_____

_____

_____

4) How do some Christians justify marriage to unbelievers as "no big deal"? What arguments do they use? What does God's Word say on the matter?

_____

_____

_____

EXPLORING THE MEANING

God hates divorce. Ezra's solution to the dire problem of intermarriage was to call on the people to divorce their unbelieving spouses. His reason for such an extreme approach was that the sin was extreme. It was intermarriage with Israel's pagan neighbors that had led God's people into the deadly sin of idolatry in the first place. Desperate circumstances sometimes call for desperate measures, and this solution may well have been the best.

Yet we must also understand that divorce is *not* God's desire for His people. Indeed, God uses strong language on the subject. "'Take heed to your spirit, and let none deal treacherously with the wife of his youth. For the LORD God of Israel says that He hates divorce, for it covers one's garment with violence,' says the LORD of hosts. 'Therefore take heed to your spirit, that you do not deal treacherously'" (Malachi 2:15–16). Notice the words that God used to describe divorce: *treachery* and *violence*. This is because when Christians divorce their spouse, they are treacherously betraying the vows they made before the Lord, and they are violently tearing asunder a couple who are one flesh.

Jesus expounded further on this subject. "Have you not read that He who made them at the beginning 'made them male and female,' and said, 'For this reason a man shall leave his father and mother and be joined to his wife, and the two shall become one flesh'? So then, they are no longer two but one flesh. Therefore what God has joined together, let not man separate" (Matthew 19:4–6). Jesus did make an exception in the case of an adulterous spouse, who has already been treacherous and violent toward the sacred union. As a general rule for believers, however, divorce is not God's plan.

Christians should not marry unbelievers. To the modern reader, Ezra's reaction to the Jews marrying foreign women might seem extreme. However, we must take care not to thrust modern sensibilities onto the text of God's Word. Ezra's response to the situation demonstrated how seriously the Lord took the sin of intermarriage. Indeed, the fact the Jews were returning from captivity and rebuilding the temple and walls indicated that God did indeed take intermarriage seriously—for it was that very sin that had led the nation of Israel into idolatry in the first place.

The Bible refers to Christians who are married to non-Christians as being "unequally yoked." The word picture is drawn from a pair of oxen that a farmer would use to pull his plow. The two animals would be connected with a firm collar, or yoke. If the two oxen had different ideas concerning their roles as plow pullers, they would pull the plow in different directions, with one trying to go left and the other pulling toward the right. The result to the farmer and his plow is self-evident: the work would come to a standstill and the plow itself might be destroyed in the contest of wills. Paul warned clearly, "Do not be unequally yoked together with unbelievers. For what fellowship has righteousness with lawlessness? And what communion has light with darkness?" (2 Corinthians 6:14).

Two further principles are given for a Christian already married to an unbeliever. First, he or she is not permitted to seek a divorce even though the marriage is unequal because God hates divorce. "If any brother has a wife who does not believe, and she is willing to live with him, let him not divorce her. And a woman who has a husband who does not believe, if he is willing to live with her, let her not divorce him" (1 Corinthians 7:12–13). Second, if an unbeliever is married to a Christian, and the unbeliever wants a divorce, the Christian should let the unbeliever go. Paul wrote, "If the unbeliever departs, let him depart; a brother or a sister is not under bondage in such cases. But God has called us to peace" (verse 15).

A new start is not a new heart. The Jews returned to the land with such promise. They had put away their idols, and only those who wanted to work on the temple returned to the land. This was a new beginning for Israel, and the sins of the previous generations of Jews must have seemed a distant memory. Yet as soon as they were in the land, they began imitating their parents' sins. It was as if the exile had never happened!

The main lesson of Ezra (and Nehemiah, Haggai, and Zechariah) is that apart from the new covenant, true obedience to God's Word is impossible. The Israelite history bears testimony to this fact. God repeatedly started over, and the Israelites repeatedly failed. He started over with Noah and his family, and sin gripped them immediately when they stepped off the ark. He started over with Moses and a new nation fleeing Egypt, but ended up leaving every one of them (except Joshua and Caleb) to die in the wilderness. Now God had again purified Israel, removing their entire nation for seventy years, but they were back into their sinful ways again.

This illustrates the fact that a new start does not necessarily indicate a new heart. This is the lesson that Jesus gave Nicodemus, who was a leader of the Jews. Jesus told him that unless a person is born again, he cannot see the kingdom of God (see John 3:3). Nicodemus thought Jesus was telling him to start his life over, and he wondered how that was even possible. But Jesus told him that without a new heart, fresh starts would simply produce fresh failures. The

Jews were learning the lesson that they did not need their land, their temple, or their wall—what they needed was their Messiah.

REFLECTING ON THE TEXT

5) Why does God hate divorce? Why did Jesus make an exception in the case of adultery (see Matthew 5:32)? How are adultery and divorce similar?

_____

_____

_____

6) What does it mean to be unequally yoked? What can you learn about intermarriage from the "ox and plow" metaphor? How does this principle apply in other areas of life?

_____

_____

_____

7) Why did Paul counsel believers not to divorce an unbelieving spouse? What did he mean when he said, "God has called us to peace" (1 Corinthians 7:15)? How is peace an important issue in an unequal marriage?

_____

_____

_____

_____

8) Why did the Jews fall back into sin again when they returned to the land? What does this teach us about the human heart? What is the solution for their sin?

_____

_____

_____

_____

PERSONAL RESPONSE

9) How do these passages affect your views of marriage? How do they affect your views on divorce or singleness? How do these teachings apply in your own life?

_____

_____

_____

_____

10) How does living with a new nature affect your struggle with sin? Do you find yourself like the Israelites, trapped in sin, or do you experience the freedom that comes with a relationship with Jesus? Explain.

_____

_____

_____

_____

Jerusalem in Nehemiah's Time

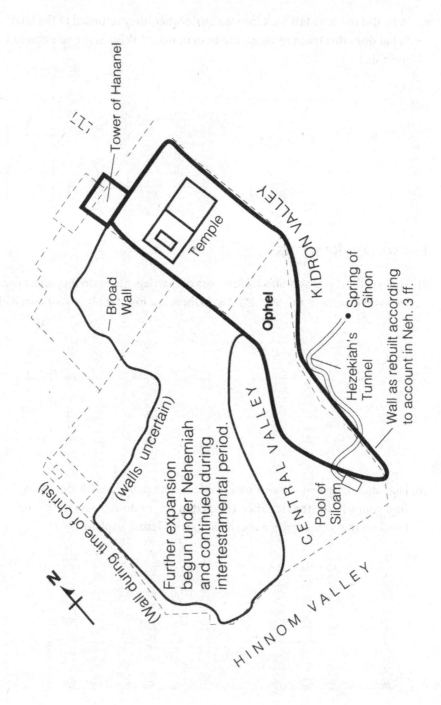

Tower of Hananel

Temple

Broad Wall

Ophel

KIDRON VALLEY

Spring of Gihon

Hezekiah's Tunnel

Wall as rebuilt according to account in Neh. 3 ff.

CENTRAL VALLEY

Pool of Siloam

(walls uncertain)

Further expansion begun under Nehemiah and continued during intertestamental period.

(Wall during time of Christ)

N

HINNOM VALLEY

8

REBUILDING THE WALL

Nehemiah 1:1–2:20

DRAWING NEAR

What are some steps governments take today when a disaster has struck an area? What are some things that get in the way of a quick rebuilding effort?

_____

_____

_____

_____

THE CONTEXT

We now move forward in time approximately 100 years to 446 BC, when a man named Nehemiah was serving King Artaxerxes of Persia. Nehemiah held an important post in the king's court as his personal cupbearer, or "food taster." He was responsible for ensuring the king did not ingest any poison, which was a fairly common way of assassinating an unpopular monarch at the time. For Nehemiah, the position came with a great degree of trust and intimacy with the king, and probably brought him great wealth, comfort, and influence at court as well.

Meanwhile, the Jews who went to Jerusalem with Zerubbabel (and their descendants) were struggling against opposition and hatred from their enemies. As we saw previously, the projected rebuilding had been halted when the enemies of the Jews successfully persuaded King Artaxerxes to forbid completion of the city wall, which was the most important part of defense for not only the temple but also the people themselves.

Judah was far away from Susa, the capital of Persia where Nehemiah served the king, and it took a full three months to travel between the two cities. Yet when Nehemiah learned of the Jews' plight, he immediately made plans to forsake his comfortable situation and join his people in their work to rebuild the wall—even at great cost to himself.

In this study, we will look at the importance of seeking God first in prayer, what it means to have a heart for the things that matter to Him, and what is required to follow His will.

KEYS TO THE TEXT

Read Nehemiah 1:1–2:20, noting the key words and phrases indicated below.

MOURNING WITH THE MOURNERS: Nehemiah, the king's cupbearer, learns of the situation in Jerusalem and responds with deep grief.

1. NEHEMIAH THE SON OF HACHALIAH: Nehemiah was the cupbearer to King Artaxerxes of Persia. His name means "Yahweh comforts." Nehemiah's father, Hachaliah, is mentioned again in Nehemiah 10:1 but nowhere else in the Old Testament.

THE TWENTIETH YEAR: This would be November–December 446 BC.

SHUSHAN THE CITADEL: This city was also known as Susa. It was located east of Babylon, approximately 150 miles north of the Persian Gulf. The book of Esther took place in this city, not long before the events of Nehemiah. Esther may well have been still alive at the time.

3. IN GREAT DISTRESS AND REPROACH: In a previous study we examined some of the distress and reproach suffered by the Jews in Jerusalem as they experienced the betrayal and opposition of the Samaritans (see Ezra 4).

Yet their suffering was greater than mere human opposition. In Nehemiah's day, pagans thought the walls and fortifications that surrounded a god's temple reflected his strength. The lack of city walls in Jerusalem reflected badly on the character of God in the eyes of Judah's neighbors, and it also left the temple unprotected against further attacks and desecration.

4. I sat down and wept: Nehemiah was deeply moved by the plight of his fellow Jews in Jerusalem. He did not just express shallow sympathy but reacted as though he were right there, in their midst, suffering with them.

fasting and praying: Nehemiah's mourning and grief were not impotent. He did not just sit in Persia's palace, wringing his hands and wondering what to do, but took action to help those who were suffering. He began with the most important and effective step: going before the Lord in prayer and fasting to seek His will and intervention.

Responding with Prayer: Nehemiah does more than sit and weep—he goes before God and asks for His help and guidance.

5. You who keep Your covenant and mercy: In this beautiful prayer, Nehemiah revealed an important fact concerning God's character: He is completely faithful to His promises. The people of Jerusalem didn't need any walls to protect the temple or themselves, for they were shielded by God's complete faithfulness (though it was still God's will for the walls to be rebuilt). Nehemiah also recognized God's absolute sovereignty over all the affairs of mankind, calling him "Lord God of heaven" who rules in the lives of kings and paupers alike.

6. I pray . . . day and night: Nehemiah prayed persistently over a period of days, not simply on this one occasion.

the children of Israel . . . my father's house and I: Notice the progression of Nehemiah's confession. He acknowledged first that his nation had sinned against the Lord by forsaking Him and pursuing false gods. He then confessed that his "father's house" had not been faithful to the Lord, which encompassed his family and those for whom he was responsible. (This might be comparable in modern times to praying for one's immediate family and local church.) Finally, he acknowledged that he was personally guilty of sin and failure before the Lord. He did not omit his own areas of culpability but recognized that his own sinful nature had contributed to the unfaithfulness of his tribe and nation. When one begins by focusing on God's faithful and holy nature, such recognition of sin—both personal and corporate—naturally follows.

8. REMEMBER, I PRAY: Nehemiah was asking the Lord to act on His promises, not suggesting that He had forgotten something. The Lord loves to have us quote His Word in an expectant way, which indicates we have read His promises and have faith that He will keep them. And He always does.

9. I WILL GATHER THEM FROM THERE: As we have already seen, the Lord had promised His people that He would scatter them to the four winds if they refused to heed His Word (see Deuteronomy 4:25–28). However, He had also promised that, at the end of seventy years, He would gather a remnant and return them to His chosen city of Jerusalem (see verses 29–31). The imagery used here is of sowing seed (which was scattered randomly by hand) and reaping a harvest. The Lord had scattered His people when they were unfaithful, but He had now reaped a harvest of obedient and loving children.

11. THE KING'S CUPBEARER: Nehemiah held one of the most trusted and intimate positions in Persia. His job was to ensure the king's safety by personally tasting his food first to make certain that no one poisoned him. This situation provided Nehemiah with a unique opportunity to speak confidentially with the king, and that was what he was preparing to do as he prayed and fasted. ("This man" refers to the king, whom Nehemiah was about to petition.)

PREPARING TO APPROACH THE KING: Nehemiah next determines to ask the king for a leave of absence—but this was a dangerous request to make.

2:1. THE MONTH OF NISAN: This would be March–April 445 BC, approximately four months since Nehemiah first learned of the situation in Jerusalem.

I TOOK THE WINE AND GAVE IT TO THE KING: Nehemiah's chief responsibility was to ensure the king's enemies did not poison him, so he was basically putting his life on the line every time he sampled the king's food and drink. This role enabled him to establish a strong bond of trust with Artaxerxes, and he would now draw on that relationship as he made his petition.

I HAD NEVER BEEN SAD IN HIS PRESENCE: Court etiquette in ancient times required that subjects appear cheerful before their king, and a sad or grim countenance could actually bring down royal wrath (see Esther 4:2). Happy subjects suggested the king was a good and wise ruler, while tears suggested otherwise. As cupbearer, Nehemiah would have needed to observe such customs of courtly behavior very carefully.

2. SINCE YOU ARE NOT SICK: The king might have been referring to Nehemiah's general state of health, which is the usual understanding here. However, he might also have been suggesting that because Nehemiah had clearly not ingested poison from the king's cup, he should be pleased. Middle Eastern monarchs in general did not take time to consider the personal lives of their subjects.

I BECAME DREADFULLY AFRAID: From a human standpoint, Nehemiah had good reason to be afraid. As already stated, it was risky business for a subject to appear unhappy in the presence of the king. But even more, Nehemiah was planning to request permission to leave the king's service, which would have been seen as a terrible insult from someone who held such a high and trusted position. He was also going to ask to rebuild the walls of Jerusalem from the very king who had ordered that building to stop. Nevertheless, Nehemiah was not acting from a human perspective, and he knew that the Lord had control over the king's decisions (see Proverbs 21:1).

4. SO I PRAYED TO THE GOD OF HEAVEN: Nehemiah was a man of prayer. He had fasted and prayed for several days prior to making his request to the king. Even now, in the midst of taking action, he was speaking to the Lord.

6. THE QUEEN ALSO SITTING BESIDE HIM: Esther had been queen of King Ahasuerus (Xerxes), who was Artaxerxes' father. It is possible that her role as the present king's stepmother had made him predisposed to show favor to the Jews—particularly if she was still alive.

WHATEVER YOU NEED: The Lord moves the king's heart to grant Nehemiah's request for a trip to Judah, and he gives him much more besides.

7. LET LETTERS BE GIVEN TO ME: These letters, which bore the royal seal of Artaxerxes, commanded all government officials to assist Nehemiah on his trip to Judah and with his work in Jerusalem. The king was effectively giving Nehemiah full authority as one of his officials in Judah.

8. HE MUST GIVE ME TIMBER: In addition to granting Nehemiah governing authority and safe passage, the king also provided much of the raw materials the Jews would need to rebuild the city gates and wall—and Nehemiah's own house as well. Lumber was a precious commodity at the time, and the ruling monarchs guarded forests carefully.

ACCORDING TO THE GOOD HAND OF MY GOD UPON ME: Nehemiah was undoubtedly grateful to King Artaxerxes for his generosity, but he recognized that his success was due solely to God's sovereign hand. It was the Lord who moved the king's heart, even after Artaxerxes had previously forbidden any such reconstruction projects in Jerusalem.

9. THE KING HAD SENT CAPTAINS OF THE ARMY AND HORSEMEN: This was a wise human precaution. It was a three-month journey from Susa to Jerusalem, and the roads along the way were fraught with banditry. The letters Nehemiah carried bore the king's seal, and as such were immensely valuable because they conferred on the bearer the full authority of the king of Persia. That alone would have put Nehemiah's life in extreme peril on such a long journey, to say nothing of the many peoples along the way who were enemies of the Jews. Yet from God's perspective, the military guard was merely superfluous. He had determined that Nehemiah should go to Jerusalem, and no power on earth could have prevented his safe arrival.

MORE OPPOSITION: *Initiating the project of rebuilding is merely a beginning. Satan's agents soon reappear to continue to oppose God's work at every step.*

10. SANBALLAT THE HORONITE AND TOBIAH THE AMMONITE: Sanballat was the governor of Samaria and probably also a Moabite—an ancient enemy of Israel. Tobiah was governor of the region east of the Jordan River, and he was an Ammonite—another ancient enemy of God's people. These two men were probably also behind the opposition against Zerubbabel that had previously stopped the work in Jerusalem.

DISTURBED THAT A MAN HAD COME: This attitude revealed the true nature of these men and their cohorts: they were committed enemies of God and His people. It is particularly revealing that they were not so much opposed to the authority that Nehemiah wielded but were opposed to anyone who sought "the well-being of the children of Israel."

12. I TOLD NO ONE: Nehemiah needed to know the current condition of the wall, what areas needed the most immediate attention, what would be required to rebuild it, and so forth. He gained this information in secret because he knew that his enemies were watching him, and he didn't know yet who could be trusted. He probably suspected that even some of the Jews in the city were

in league with Sanballat and Tobiah, so to be safe he did not even tell "the Jews, the priests, the nobles, the officials, or the others who did the work" (verse 16).

17. LET US BUILD: Nehemiah next invited all of God's people to join him in the work. It was not Nehemiah's project but the Lord's, and He had called all His children to be involved in His work. This also would enable Nehemiah to discover who was fully committed to the plans of God, as those would be the people who threw themselves into the rebuilding.

THAT WE MAY NO LONGER BE A REPROACH: This was Nehemiah's motivation in undertaking this huge project: he was concerned about the glory of God. The destruction of the temple and city of Jerusalem had made a mockery of God's name in the eyes of Judah's enemies, so Nehemiah called on the people of God to restore His glory to the world around them.

18. I TOLD THEM OF THE HAND OF MY GOD: It is good to tell others of the ways God has blessed you and how you have seen Him working faithfully in your own life. This encourages others who might be facing discouragement, and it brings glory to God's name.

UNLEASHING THE TEXT

1) Why was Nehemiah so upset when he learned of the plight of the Jews in Jerusalem? What was his response?

_____

_____

_____

2) What was the "great distress and reproach" that the Jews were facing in Judah? In what ways did this reflect on God's glory?

_____

_____

_____

3) Why did Nehemiah survey the wall around Jerusalem in secret? Why did he then call the people to join him in the rebuilding? What does his example teach about leadership?

_____

_____

_____

4) What can you learn about prayer from Nehemiah's example (see Nehemiah 1:5–11)?

_____

_____

_____

EXPLORING THE MEANING

Service is crucial, especially when it's costly. Nehemiah lived in Persia, the greatest and wealthiest nation of its day. Furthermore, he lived in Susa, the nation's capital and one of the richest and most comfortable of the Persian cities. To top this off, he was the cupbearer to the king himself, a position of high trust and influence. He was undoubtedly rich and high in the ranks of the most powerful nation on earth. Jerusalem was far away—a journey of three full months. It would have been easy for Nehemiah to forget about his people.

Yet when he heard about the plight of his fellow Jews in far-off Judah, he mourned, wept, fasted, and prayed. What's more, he determined in his heart to forsake all the blessings and comforts of Persia and exchange them for hard work, rough living conditions, and constant hatred and opposition from God's enemies. In fact, Nehemiah was so determined to help with the work in Jerusalem that he risked his own life to get there. He put himself in peril of the king's wrath by making the request to leave the king's service, and then he embarked on the dangerous and uncomfortable trip to Judah.

It was not wrong or sinful for Nehemiah to enjoy the comforts of Persia and the king's court. The Lord had placed him in this position, and Nehemiah was being faithful to the tasks God had given him. But the Lord had placed him there specifically so that he might be positioned to help the Jews at this moment of crisis, just as He had placed Esther where she could save the Jews from annihilation a generation earlier (see Esther 4:14). The Lord was calling Nehemiah to voluntarily forsake all these blessings to participate in an important project, and the blessings that came from his obedience far surpassed all the comforts of the king's palace. When the Lord calls us in a similar way, we must always heed the call, for our obedience will bring glory to His name and great blessings to us.

Our protection is found in God alone. The Jews in Jerusalem were anxious to rebuild the city walls. They wanted a strong defense against the many enemies who surrounded them and would have been glad to see them carried off into captivity once again. King Artaxerxes himself recognized the danger in the region, which is why he provided Nehemiah with a powerful military escort to protect him on the dangerous journey. These were treacherous times for the Jews, for there were many who hated them and longed to participate in their destruction.

Yet the Lord did not need stone walls or well-armed soldiers to protect His people. His omnipotent hand was sufficient, and His faithfulness to His promises ensured that nothing could ever touch His servants without His permission. Ezra had previously chosen to trust in the Lord's protection and make the same long journey without any military escort (see Ezra 8:22)—and his faith had proved sound. This does not mean, of course, that Nehemiah had less faith than Ezra. The king had offered the escort, and Nehemiah saw that as God's provision at the time. Nevertheless, had the king *not* offered any soldiers, Nehemiah would still have arrived safely through the Lord's faithfulness.

However, we must not overlook the important element of obedience in the Lord's protection. Notice what Nehemiah prayed in 1:5-6: "O great and awesome God, You who keep Your covenant and mercy with those who love You and observe Your commandments, please let Your ear be attentive and Your eyes open." The Lord is always faithful to His promises, and faithful to protect His children from the enemy, but He also expects us to be faithful to

His Word. When we sin, we make ourselves vulnerable to the attacks of the evil one and hinder God's hand of blessing in our lives. Our job is to obey His Word and trust Him for our needs.

God loves to see the faith of His people. When Nehemiah spent time in fasting and prayer before approaching the king with his risky request, he reminded God of the promises he had made concerning Judah. He pointed out that the Lord had kept His promise to send the people into captivity if they persisted in idolatry, and he then reminded God of His further promise to return them to Judah after seventy years. He was reminding the Lord of these things not out of a spirit of accusation but in a spirit of expectation.

There is another layer to this prayer, however, which we might easily overlook. In order for Nehemiah to remind God of His promises, he had to *know* those promises in the first place. Nehemiah's knowledge of the limitation on the captivity indicated that he had spent time reading and meditating on the Word of God. This is one reason why the Lord is pleased when we quote His Word to Him in prayer, because He wants us to read it, memorize it, and meditate on it. But He also wants us to make His Word part of our own lives and ask ourselves how it applies to us personally in our daily routines.

It is good for us to remind the Lord of the promises He has made to us. Of course, the Lord will keep His promises even if we do not remind him of them, simply because He never fails. Yet He delights when His children remind Him of His Word, because it shows that we have faith in His character and His faithfulness. It also strengthens us and deepens our faith when we remind *ourselves* of His promises.

REFLECTING ON THE TEXT

5) What risks did Nehemiah take to help the Jews in Judah? What were his motivations in taking these risks? What would you have done in his situation?

_____

_____

_____

6) Why did Ezra not take a military escort on his trip to Judah (see Ezra 8:22)? Why did Nehemiah accept the king's guard on this trip? What do these men's attitudes reveal about God's protection?

_____

_____

_____

_____

7) Why did Nehemiah remind God of His promises in his prayer? What effect might this have had on Nehemiah? How do these principles apply to your prayer life?

_____

_____

_____

_____

8) What did Nehemiah tell the people in Jerusalem after he surveyed the wall (see Nehemiah 2:18)? How did the people respond? How might these insights apply to your witness for Christ?

_____

_____

_____

_____

PERSONAL RESPONSE

9) What are you presently depending on for your security? In what areas of your life might you need to place more faith in God's protection?

_____

_____

_____

_____

10) When has another Christian served you at great cost to himself or herself? Why did he or she do so? Who might be the one the Lord is calling you to serve this week?

_____

_____

_____

_____

9

THE OPPOSITION INCREASES

Nehemiah 3:1–4:23

DRAWING NEAR

What tends to happen to people's enthusiasm for a project when it drags on longer than they expected or they encounter problems they didn't expect?

_____

_____

_____

THE CONTEXT

Nehemiah had made the arduous journey from Susa to Jerusalem, had personally surveyed the damage to the city wall, and had called on the officials of the city to join with him in the rebuilding effort. The people had responded in faith, committed themselves to the project, and set to work on the walls and gates with great vigor and zeal. Through the Lord's blessing and help, they made good progress, and soon the wall was nearly half built.

When Sanballat, Tobiah, and Geshem—the leaders of those who opposed the Jews—observed the people's progress, they laughed and said, "What is this thing that you are doing? Will you rebel against the king?" Nehemiah responded by telling them the God of heaven Himself would guide and prosper their efforts. He added, "You have no heritage or right or memorial in Jerusalem" (Nehemiah 2:19–20).

In this study, we will find these enemies responding with as much zeal and vigor to *halt* the rebuilding as the Jews have shown in pursuing the work. They will stop at nothing to prevent the completion of the walls and will resort to all forms of verbal abuse and scandal—all while planning a mass murder of the Jews. Nehemiah will demonstrate that God's people must expect opposition and always be prepared to face it.

The most important lesson we will gain from this study is that we must always trust in God's promises as we accomplish the tasks that He has given to us to complete. As we lean on His strength and depend on His provision, we will see Him come through in miraculous ways.

KEYS TO THE TEXT

Read Nehemiah 3:1–4:23, noting the key words and phrases indicated below.

DIVIDE AND CONQUER: *The reconstruction effort begins in Jerusalem, with different groups assuming responsibility for the repairs on different parts of the wall and gates.*

3:1. ELIASHIB THE HIGH PRIEST: He was the grandson of Jeshua, the high priest from Zerubbabel's era (see Ezra 2:2). The events in this chapter took place on the fourth day of the Hebrew month of Ab (July–August) in 445 BC.

THE SHEEP GATE: This gate was located in the northeast section of Jerusalem. The narrative moves around the perimeter of Jerusalem in a counterclockwise direction.

TOWER OF THE HUNDRED . . . TOWER OF HANANEL. This northern section of Jerusalem opened up to the central Benjamin plateau, where enemy forces could attack most easily from the north. The rest of the perimeter of the city was protected by the natural valley topography.

3. FISH GATE: So named because merchants sold fish on the northern side of Jerusalem. The people of Tyre and other coastal towns routinely brought fish to sell.

5. THEIR NOBLES DID NOT PUT THEIR SHOULDERS TO THE WORK OF THEIR LORD: One explanation for this, beyond just the laziness of the rich

people in the city, is that these nobles had been pledged to Tobiah for personal gain.

6. THE OLD GATE: This is believed to have been in the northwest corner of Jerusalem.

8. THE BROAD WALL: Located on the western side of the northern sector.

11. TOWER OF THE OVENS: Located on the western side of Jerusalem.

13. THE VALLEY GATE: Located on the western side of Jerusalem.

14. THE REFUSE GATE: Also known as the Dung Gate. A common sewer ran to the Kidron Brook into the Valley of Hinnom at the southern tip of the city.

15. THE FOUNTAIN GATE: Located on the southeast corner of Jerusalem.

THE KING'S GARDEN: Located in the southeast sector.

16. TOMBS OF DAVID: Presumably located in the southeast sector.

HOUSE OF THE MIGHTY: This location probably was associated with David's mighty men (see 2 Samuel 23:8–39).

19. THE ARMORY: Located on the eastern side of Jerusalem.

26. WHO DWELT IN OPHEL: An area located south of the temple mount, near the Water Gate, where the Nethinim lived.

THE WATER GATE: Located south of Gihon Spring on the east side of Jerusalem.

28. THE HORSE GATE: Located in the eastern sector.

29. THE EAST GATE: Possibly located to the east of the temple mount.

31. THE MIPHKAD GATE: Located in the northeast sector.

32. THE SHEEP GATE: Having traveled around Jerusalem in a counterclockwise direction, the narrative ends where it began.

MOCKERY AND DISDAIN: The enemies of God's people see the progress the Jews are making on the walls and gates of Jerusalem and are filled with fury.

4:1. FURIOUS AND VERY INDIGNANT: On the surface, Sanballat, the governor of Samaria, was outraged that the Jews had overridden his authority in the region by gaining the support of the king. But the deeper truth is that he was an enemy of God—and therefore an enemy of God's people. He could not abide the thought that the Jews were going to prosper and rebuild their beloved city of Jerusalem.

2. HE SPOKE BEFORE HIS BRETHREN: For mockery to have any effect requires a sympathetic audience, so Sanballat attempted to draw others into his plans to belittle the Jews. His "brethren" would have been others of like mind who hated God's people as well. It is possible that he also intended to provoke "the army of Samaria" into action, as that would have swiftly brought the Persian overlord down on Samaria. Harassment and mockery would prove to be the primary strategy the enemy would use to prevent the reconstruction of the walls.

4. HEAR, O OUR GOD: Once again, Nehemiah's first response to the danger and opposition was to bow down before the Lord in prayer. Notice that Nehemiah did not respond to the taunts and mockery of his enemies. Instead, he poured out his heart to the Lord and allowed God to deal with the opposition.

5. DO NOT COVER THEIR INIQUITY: Nehemiah was acknowledging that his enemies were attacking God rather than him. It was the Lord whom they despised, and Nehemiah was calling on Him to defend His glory before the world. Nehemiah recognized that forgiveness is granted not to those who oppose the will of God but to those who eagerly submit to His will.

6. SO WE BUILT THE WALL: Nehemiah effectively turned the situation over to the Lord in his short prayer, and then he returned his focus to the work the Lord had given him. He did not pretend the opposition did not exist, but he did trust that God would be their defender.

THE PEOPLE HAD A MIND TO WORK: The people had been enthusiastic and eager to participate during the early phases of the building project. They had divided the work among themselves and been excited to see the progress as the wall came together. However, human nature tends to cause people to lose enthusiasm as time passes—and the taunts of the enemy were not helping to keep the people motivated. It is during such times in our own lives that determination becomes important in obeying and completing the Lord's work, for distractions and discouragement will multiply as our enthusiasm dissipates.

ENEMIES ON ALL SIDES: Groups of people who would not normally be allies with each other now band together on all four sides of Jerusalem to hinder God's work.

7. THE ARABS, THE AMMONITES, AND THE ASHDODITES: The Samaritans (under Sanballat) were to the north, the Arabs (under Geshem) were

located to the south, and the Ammonites (under Tobiah) were to the east. Added to the list of enemies were the dwellers of Ashdod to the west—thus effectively surrounding the people of God on every side. Apparently, the Ashdodites had come to the point where they were at least contemplating a full-scale attack on Jerusalem because of the rapid progress of the wall. Ironically, these groups would not have cooperated under normal circumstances—what drew them into this alliance was a mutual hatred of God and His people. This same trend can be seen today in parts of the Middle East.

THEY BECAME VERY ANGRY: Here the enemies tipped their hand, showing the true nature of their opposition. They had pretended to care about the king's taxes and about national security, and had acted as if the Jews could not construct anything lasting, but in the end they were only angry at the thought of the Jews being able to defend themselves. God's enemies criticize, manipulate, and persecute God's people today just as they did then.

8. CREATE CONFUSION: Another of the devil's favorite tactics is to create confusion and chaos wherever unity exists among God's people. For this reason it is not uncommon for the people of God to be tempted toward disunity, especially during times of critical work on behalf of the Lord. The enemies of the Jews did not care what the people believed. They simply wanted to stop the progress being made on rebuilding the wall.

9. WE MADE OUR PRAYER . . . WE SET A WATCH: Note the people's two-fold approach to the danger they faced: they turned to God in prayer, and they took steps to guard themselves. The Jews recognized their protection was from God alone, yet that did not exempt them from carrying out their basic human responsibilities. It would have been negligent not to establish watchmen to guard the wall (and their homes) at night. The Lord wants His children to trust Him for their security, but He also expects them to be responsible.

DISCOURAGEMENT AND VIOLENCE: God's enemies now resort to threats of murder, and the Jews begin to grow weary and discouraged.

10. THE STRENGTH OF THE LABORERS IS FAILING: The Jews' initial enthusiasm had worn off and fatigue was setting in. This was a critical point in Nehemiah's administration, for the enemy's attacks were beginning to have their desired effect of halting the work. Nehemiah needed to take steps to renew the people's enthusiasm for the project to be a success.

so much rubbish: This term literally means *dust*. The people were referring to the rubble or ruins of the prior destruction (in 586 BC), which they had to clear away before they could make significant progress on rebuilding the walls.

11. kill them and cause the work to cease: Part of the strategy of the enemy coalition was to frighten and intimidate the Jews by making them think an army would surprise them with a massive force that would engulf them. God's enemies will stop at nothing, even mass murder, in hopes of preventing the fulfillment of His plans. This is a futile hope, however, as nothing whatsoever can prevent God's plans from coming to pass. The destruction His enemies plan will come on their own heads (see Proverbs 26:27).

12. the Jews who dwelt near them: These were Jews who had not gotten involved in the rebuilding project. They probably meant well by warning the others of an impending attack. However, they had inadvertently become tools of the enemies by yielding to fear and potentially spreading that fear to the people who were actually working. As we have seen throughout this study, fear is the enemy of God's people.

FOILED AGAIN: The Lord prevents His enemies from attacking His people during the work of rebuilding, for the battle belongs to Him alone.

13. Therefore I positioned men: God had exposed Sanballat's strategy of mustering the army of Samaria by revealing it to the nearby Jews so they would report it to Judah's leaders. Although Nehemiah and those he led were vigilant, armed, and ready, they consistently gave God the glory for their victories and construction successes.

14. Do not be afraid of them: Once again we are given this important injunction to not be afraid. God continually tells His people not to yield to fear because fear leads a person away from God rather than toward Him.

Remember the Lord . . . and fight: Here again we see Nehemiah taking both a spiritual and practical approach to the problem. Remembering the Lord involves meditating on His Word and His character as well as turning to Him in prayer. The fighting that Nehemiah had in mind was quite literal, as demonstrated by the Jews' willingness to take up arms to defend themselves.

15. GOD HAD BROUGHT THEIR PLOT TO NOTHING: Nehemiah never lost sight of the fact that God was in control of all events. The plot was not foiled because the Jews had learned about it, nor because of their readiness to fight back, but because God prevented it.

16. HELD THE SPEARS, THE SHIELDS, THE BOWS, AND WORE ARMOR: Notice that half of these weapons were offensive (spears and bows) and half were defensive (shields and armor). Paul would later use such military weaponry to describe the Christian life, including the shield of faith, the breastplate of righteousness, and "the sword of the Spirit, which is the word of God" (Ephesians 6:14–17). Yet on a practical level, Nehemiah took strong precautions to guard against the threatened physical attack of the enemy by dividing the workers into two teams. One team would guard while the other team worked. The effect of the threats, however, was to cut the work force in half, and even those who worked carried weapons in case of attack.

18. THE ONE WHO SOUNDED THE TRUMPET: Among other functions, the trumpet would have sounded a loud call to arms that alerted all the Jews of an attack. Nehemiah kept a trumpeter at his side always so the alarm could be sounded immediately. He took it on himself, as the Lord's appointed leader, to stand guard vigilantly on behalf of those under his leadership.

20. OUR GOD WILL FIGHT FOR US: Once again, Nehemiah reminded his coworkers that the battle belonged to the Lord, not to the strength of their arms.

UNLEASHING THE TEXT

1) How did Nehemiah divide the work on the city walls and gates? What were some of the benefits in adopting this approach?

_____

_____

_____

_____

_____

2) What tactics did the enemies use to thwart the rebuilding project? How do God's enemies today use similar tactics?

_____

_____

_____

3) Why did Nehemiah command his workers to always be armed? What effect did this have on the work? What effect did it have on the enemies?

_____

_____

_____

4) What role did prayer play in the events of this chapter? What practical steps did the people take? How does a Christian blend prayer and practical common sense?

_____

_____

_____

EXPLORING THE MEANING

Expect opposition, but don't ignore it. Zerubbabel, Ezra, and Nehemiah all faced determined opposition from powerful foes. They understood that life is filled with spiritual battles, for the enemy of our souls continuously strives to hinder the work of God. These men expected opposition to the Lord's great project of rebuilding Jerusalem, and they were not caught off guard when it came. We must not assume every hardship, opposition, or obstacle is an indication that we are acting according to the Lord's will. God *does* use practical hindrances at times to force us to recognize when we are not going in the right direction.

Consider Balaam, for example, a pagan shaman who practiced sorcery and other wicked acts for profit. He had been offered a great sum of money to cast a curse on the Lord's people after their exodus from Egypt, but the Lord had warned him, "You shall not go . . . you shall not curse the people, for they are blessed" (Numbers 22:12). Nevertheless, Balaam saddled his donkey and headed out—ostensibly to bless God's people, yet in disobedience to the Lord's command. As he traveled along, the Lord sent an angel to hinder his donkey's progress. He even caused the donkey to speak (who showed more wisdom than his foolish master) in order to warn Balaam that he was going the wrong way.

When we do the Lord's work, we will face spiritual opposition from the enemies of God's people, and we must expect it. But when there's any doubt, we shouldn't assume that opposition is a "green light" on our actions. Rather, we must turn immediately to the Lord in prayer and meditate on His Word. The Lord never commands His people to do anything contrary to the principles of Scripture, and He might be using obstacles to open our eyes to a wrong decision.

When enemies assail you, talk to the Lord. The Jews faced a variety of threats and opposition from their enemies as they were rebuilding the wall. They were openly mocked and derided, falsely accused of evil motives and rebellious plans, subtly infiltrated by men who sought to discourage them and hinder their work, and even threatened with murder. However, in every instance under Nehemiah's leadership, we see God's people turning to the Lord in prayer and expecting to find their safety and security in Him.

This is an excellent example that Christians would do well to follow. Most of us instinctively try to resolve problems on our own, either by trying to devise our own schemes and solutions, or by simply running away. However, notice how Nehemiah responded to those who were mocking him and slandering his reputation. He did not defend himself, nor did he retaliate with sarcasm and verbal abuse. When those same enemies planned to attack the Jews violently, Nehemiah did not strike out with his own sword. In both cases, the Lord's people turned to their God in prayer.

Turning to God in prayer is not the same as abdicating responsibility. We still need to fulfill our responsibilities—as the next principle will illustrate—and one of those responsibilities is to use common sense while not giving in to fear and discouragement. But in the big picture, the battle belongs to the Lord, and we are wise to turn the fighting over to Him.

We must be alert and prepared for battle. Nehemiah didn't take the enemy's threat lightly when he learned they were planning to slaughter the Jews. He knew, of course, that the true protection of God's people lay solely in God's hands, but he also understood that he had a responsibility for the safety and welfare of those under his authority. Consequently, he took strong steps to prepare for the threat of battle. What's more, he expected all those working on the Lord's project to also remain alert and well armed. It must have been a real hindrance to the work of building, which was strenuous enough without having only one hand available, but Nehemiah felt the work of self-defense was as important as the work of rebuilding the wall.

Most of us do not face the threat of physical violence for our faith (though there are many Christians in parts of the world who do), but this principle applies at least as much on the spiritual level. Even if our neighbors are not threatening to attack us, we all face an enemy who is deadlier than those who opposed the Jews. For this reason, God commands us through His Word to be constantly on guard against the forces of wickedness, and He also commands us to go everywhere well armed. As Paul instructs, we are to carry with us "the sword of the Spirit, which is the word of God" (Ephesians 6:17). The writer of Hebrews gives this further detail: "For the word of God is living and powerful, and sharper than any two-edged sword, piercing even to the division of soul and spirit, and of joints and marrow, and is a discerner of the thoughts and intents of the heart" (Hebrews 4:12).

Well-armed and vigilant Christians spend time reading and meditating daily on the Word of God. And like all well-trained soldiers, believers in Christ also stay in close contact with the Commanding Officer through prayer and obedience. The military analogy, in fact, is apt in life, because we live in a battle zone where the enemy is constantly trying to destroy us. Therefore, we must always "be sober, be vigilant; because your adversary the devil walks about like a roaring lion, seeking whom he may devour. Resist him, steadfast in the faith, knowing that the same sufferings are experienced by your brotherhood in the world" (1 Peter 5:8–9).

Reflecting on the Text

5) Why did Nehemiah ask the Lord to not cover the iniquity of his enemies (see Nehemiah 4:5)? How is this different from harboring a vindictive spirit?

_____

_____

_____

_____

6) What does it mean to resist the devil (see 1 Peter 5:9)? How is this done, in practical terms?

_____

_____

_____

_____

7) Why did Nehemiah make no response to the verbal abuse of the enemies? Why did he make a practical response to their threats of violence? In what circumstances is each response most wise?

_____

_____

_____

_____

8) When have you faced opposition or problems caused by an enemy? When has the Lord used difficulties to turn you away from doing wrong? How can you tell the difference?

_____

_____

_____

PERSONAL RESPONSE

9) How do you normally respond to threats or verbal abuse? How did Jesus respond to such things? In what ways do you need to become more like Him?

_____

_____

_____

10) What trials or hardships are you trying to resolve in your own strength? List them below, and then spend time each day this week asking the Lord to take over the battles.

_____

_____

_____

_____

10

LEADING BY EXAMPLE
Nehemiah 5:1–6:19

DRAWING NEAR

What does it mean to "practice what you preach"? Why is it important for a person in leadership to exhibit this trait?

_____

_____

_____

THE CONTEXT

Even though Nehemiah's workforce had essentially been cut in half—with half the men working while the other half stayed on security duty—progress on the wall continued. Yet at the end of a typical day, Nehemiah's workers had neither the time nor energy left to attend to many of their own personal responsibilities. Many of those responsibilities were important, such as paying their taxes and gathering enough food to feed their families.

This led many of the people into financial difficulties. They had debts that could not be paid right away, or they had to borrow to pay their taxes. Some of them had to go outside the city to work as hired hands harvesting other people's crops. Many people in Jerusalem and the surrounding areas were going hungry, and they ended up being exploited by those who were more fortunate.

The Lord had given clear instructions to His people on how to be generous with the poor. However, Nehemiah discovered that despite the work on the wall and the temple, the people were not obeying the laws that God had given Israel. In spite of the new start in the land, many Jews were still reluctant to live in the way God had instructed, and they were taking unfair advantage of the poor for personal gain.

KEYS TO THE TEXT

Read Nehemiah 5:1–6:19, noting the key words and phrases indicated below.

> THE PEOPLE CRY OUT: *Work on the wall is suddenly interrupted by a great outcry from the people. They cannot pay their bills, and they are being sold into slavery.*

5:1. THERE WAS A GREAT OUTCRY: Notice the outcry was from "the people and their wives," which suggests entire families of workers had been affected. The sad irony is that the outcry was "against their Jewish brethren." The workers had no complaint against the Persian government (indeed, they had reason to be grateful to the king), nor against the foreigners in their midst. The problem came from the Jews themselves, for the wealthy were taking advantage of those doing the rebuilding. These may have been the same Jews who earlier refused to join the work of rebuilding, probably having formed an alliance with Sanballat and Tobias.

2. LET US GET GRAIN: There were three groups facing financial crisis. The first group had spent all their time and energy rebuilding the wall and had no time left to work for their own food. These people may have been among the poorest—those who owned no property and normally would have earned a living by harvesting the fields of others.

3. WE HAVE MORTGAGED OUR LANDS: The second group consisted of property owners who had been forced to take mortgages in order to pay their bills. To make matters worse, there had been a famine, and these people were having trouble feeding their families.

4. WE HAVE BORROWED MONEY FOR THE KING'S TAX: The third group had been hard hit with Persian taxes both on property and on produce. This group was the hardest hit, for they had not only mortgaged their lands but also sold their children into slavery.

5. FORCING OUR SONS AND OUR DAUGHTERS TO BE SLAVES: People who could not pay their debts might sell themselves (or their children) into slavery. God's Word contains specific stipulations concerning this practice— stipulations these wealthy Jews were not obeying. First, the Lord forbade His people to charge interest to one another on loans (see Exodus 22:25). Second, the debtor was to be treated with dignity and respect as a fellow member of God's chosen people (see Leviticus 25:39–40). Third, such debts might include indentured service, but it did *not* include a person's property. The Lord had given the Promised Land to all His people, and they were not permitted to buy or sell that land, even to one another (see Numbers 36:7–9).

NOT IN OUR POWER TO REDEEM THEM: Even the indentured servant-hood was limited to seven years, after which the entire debt was to be canceled and the servants returned to their homes and families. (There was also a special Year of Jubilee every fifty years in which all debts were automatically canceled.) Neglecting this was one of the sins that had brought on the exile, and the Jews had already returned to it.

RIGHTEOUS INDIGNATION: Nehemiah responds to this situation with great anger, but his actions in response are somewhat surprising.

6. I BECAME VERY ANGRY: Nehemiah demonstrated the difference between sinful anger and righteous indignation. His anger was kindled by the fact that the Jews were not obeying God's Word. However, he did not express his anger in retaliation but instead addressed the underlying sinful behavior that was causing the problem.

7. I REBUKED THE NOBLES AND RULERS: Nehemiah took time to reflect and seek the Lord's wisdom in how to handle the situation before rebuking the nobles and rulers. The commitment of this group to the reconstruction project had been negligible, and their loyalty to the Jews' enemies had added to their opportunistic attitudes, which placed them close to the status of opposition. They had become the enemy from within. The Hebrew phrase here for

rebuke implies a strong contention, even taking legal action against someone. Nehemiah did not overreact, but he did not gloss over the nobles' and rulers' sin either.

8. WE HAVE REDEEMED OUR JEWISH BRETHREN: Once again, Nehemiah set an example by his own behavior. He first denounced with just severity the evil conduct of selling a brother by means of usury. Nehemiah then contrasted it with his action of redeeming (with his own money) some of the Jewish exiles who through debt had lost their freedom in Babylon.

THEY WERE SILENCED: Nehemiah's rebuke was unanswerable because he had founded it on two things: God's Word and his own personal example. The fact that he had obeyed the Lord at cost to himself in a similar matter left no room for his opponents to argue back.

9. BECAUSE OF THE REPROACH OF THE NATIONS: Once again, Nehemiah's paramount concern was the glory of God before the rest of the world. The actions of these nobles and rulers had placed their fellow Jews in danger, but it was far worse that they had slandered God's name before their pagan neighbors.

NEHEMIAH'S STAND: Nehemiah continues to lead by example by refusing to accept provisions that were lawfully due to him in order to avoid further burdens on the people.

10. I . . . AM LENDING THEM MONEY AND GRAIN: Nehemiah expected God's people to lend to those in need without expectation of profit. If a person was destitute, those who had the means were to give to them as a free gift. If the debtor was able to repay the money, no interest was to be charged. Such generosity was a mark of true godliness (see Psalm 15:1–5).

11. RESTORE NOW TO THEM: Nehemiah commanded those who had taken advantage of their brethren to restore all the property they had confiscated and to restore all the interest they had charged. He called the people to obey the Lord's commands, but he did not go beyond that to mete out punishment against those who had disobeyed. Once they had restored what they had taken, he considered the matter to be closed.

14. NEITHER I NOR MY BROTHERS ATE THE GOVERNOR'S PROVISIONS: Nehemiah was entitled to collect taxes from the people in Judah because he had been officially appointed as the king's representative. Yet he didn't. He

refrained from taxing the Jews in order to serve as an example to them of self-sacrificial love.

16. I ALSO CONTINUED THE WORK ON THIS WALL: Nehemiah dealt with issues that came up, but his central focus was always on completing the work the Lord had called him to do. He was not there for personal profit, and he did not waste his time buying land or striving to further his career. He was there to build the wall . . . and build he did.

17. AT MY TABLE: Nehemiah's role as governor carried certain social obligations, just as any important political official is expected to entertain influential guests today. The costs were quite high for such obligations, and previous governors had not hesitated to make the Jews pay the bill through taxes. But Nehemiah met his obligations out of his own pocket, refusing to add to the financial burden of his fellow Jews.

AN OPEN LETTER: The enemies of the Jews have been unable to stop the work through the threat of military force, so now they turn to more subtle means.

6:2. SENT TO ME: This suggests that a messenger had delivered either a letter or an oral message to Nehemiah. Sanballat, Tobiah, Geshem, and the others had evidently realized they could not prevent Nehemiah's project from succeeding by open military engagement, so they now attempted to overcome him by deception.

IN THE PLAIN OF ONO: This plain was located south of Joppa on the western extremity of Judah along the seacoast.

3. SO I SENT MESSENGERS: Nehemiah knew his enemies were luring him into a trap, so he sent representatives to meet with them. This action itself was risky, as these representatives themselves might have been killed or imprisoned for ransom.

5. OPEN LETTER: Official letters were typically rolled up and sealed with an official signet by the letter's sender or one of his assisting officials. An open or unsealed letter was not only a sign of disrespect and open criticism but also suggested the information therein was public knowledge. The goal of this document was to intimidate Nehemiah into stopping the work.

6. IT IS REPORTED AMONG THE NATIONS: The letter suggested that Nehemiah's intent to revolt was common knowledge that would get back to the

king of Persia if he did not come to the requested conference. This information, had it been true, would have brought Persian troops against the Jews. Even though Judah had a reputation for breaking its allegiances with its overlord kings, on this occasion that was not the case.

THAT YOU MAY BE THEIR KING: As we have seen, Artaxerxes had commissioned the rebuilding of the wall based on his relationship of trust with Nehemiah. Once the project was accomplished, the king expected Nehemiah to return to Susa. These allegations that Nehemiah was fortifying the city so he might be made king would seriously violate the Persian king's trust—if not create a war. The plot was an attempt to intimidate Nehemiah with the idea that a wedge was being driven between him and Artaxerxes. In this way they hoped to provoke Nehemiah to come to the meeting—which would have resulted in his death.

7. APPOINTED PROPHETS TO PROCLAIM: If there were such prophets, Sanballat had actually hired them to feed incorrect information, thus generating the false rumor. By dispatching such prophets to make public proclamations that Nehemiah had made himself king, he hoped to make it appear that the Jews were supplanting the Persian imperial rule.

10. SECRET INFORMER: When the letter failed to intimidate Nehemiah, his enemies decided to try intimidation from within. They hired a false prophet named Shemaiah to tell Nehemiah there was a plot against his life in an effort to lure him into the Holy Place in the temple. For Nehemiah to enter and shut himself in the Holy Place would have been a desecration of the house of God and would have caused people to question his reverence for God.

THE WALL IS COMPLETED: In spite of all the enemies' tactics and strategies, the work on the wall continues and is actually completed in just fifty-two days.

15. TWENTY-FIFTH DAY OF ELUL: The wall was finished in August–September of 445 BC.

16. THIS WORK WAS DONE BY OUR GOD: While modern readers might be tempted to exalt the leadership qualities that brought the work to completion, Nehemiah viewed it as a result of the work God had done among them. God works through faithful people, but it is God who works.

17. THE NOBLES OF JUDAH SENT MANY LETTERS TO TOBIAH: Nehemiah added a footnote that in the days of building the wall, the nobles of Judah

who refused to work were actually in alliance and correspondence with Tobiah, because—though his ancestors were Ammonites—he had married into a respectable Jewish family.

18. MANY IN JUDAH WERE PLEDGED TO HIM: According to Nehemiah 13:4, the high priest, Eliashib, was allied with Tobiah. The meddling of these nobles, by trying to play both sides through reports to Tobiah and to Nehemiah, had only widened the breach as Tobiah had escalated the efforts to frighten Nehemiah.

UNLEASHING THE TEXT

1) What financial crisis befell the laborers in Jerusalem? What caused it? How had they become vulnerable to such a crisis?

_____

_____

_____

2) How did God expect the nobles to respond to the needs of their brethren? Why do you think the Jewish leaders did not follow God's Law?

_____

_____

_____

3) What tactics did Sanballat, Tobiah, Geshem, and the other enemies employ to stop the work? How did Nehemiah respond to each attack against him?

_____

_____

_____

4) In what ways did Nehemiah demonstrate the qualities of a strong, godly leader in this passage? What leaders have you known who were like him?

_____

_____

_____

EXPLORING THE MEANING

God is compassionate, particularly toward the poor. Many people often assume the Old Testament describes God as being wrathful and vengeful. However, the most common word used in the Old Testament to describe God is _compassionate_. God cares about people, and He particularly cares about the poor and needy who belong to Him. In this case, the poor who were being exploited were the ones who had thrown themselves wholeheartedly into the work of rebuilding the walls and had stood firm in spite of opposition.

These individuals had demonstrated a strong commitment to the Lord's work, and one would have expected their fellow Jews to be grateful. Unfortunately, they were not rewarded with gratitude but were exploited. The nobles and rulers who were taking advantage of them assumed that God simply would not notice or not care about this exploitation of the weak. These were powerful and influential men—with money and property—who had the capability of taking advantage of an opportunity and did not hesitate to do so. These men had forgotten that because God is compassionate, he hears the cry of the oppressed (see Exodus 22:27).

The Lord calls His people to be generous with those who are less fortunate and give freely with no expectation of repayment. Solomon wrote, "He who has pity on the poor lends to the LORD, and He will pay back what he has given" (Proverbs 19:17). Jesus gave us practical instruction on how to do this: "Give to everyone who asks of you. And from him who takes away your goods do not ask them back. And just as you want men to do to you, you also do to them likewise. . . . Love your enemies, do good, and lend, hoping for nothing in return; and your reward will be great, and you will be sons of the Most High. For He is kind to the unthankful and evil. Therefore be merciful, just as your Father also is merciful" (Luke 6:30–31, 35–36).

A godly leader leads by example. Nehemiah was a great leader. He organized more than one trip from Persia to Judah, gathering all the materials and resources needed to undertake the mighty work of rebuilding the city walls. He also governed with wisdom, leading God's people through some difficult circumstances. But one of the strongest elements of his leadership was his own life, as he demonstrated through his own example what it meant to be a godly man.

When some of the people sinned and took advantage of their brothers, Nehemiah took a firm stand by confronting the wrongdoers and leading them back into obedience. The key word, however, is *leading*. Nehemiah did not *force* them into submission but *led* them into godliness through his own example. Nehemiah not only told the nobles and rulers to stop charging usury but also demonstrated the right way to give generously and lend freely. He set that example *before* it became a problem among the people.

A good teacher does not simply give lectures on how to master a skill but also demonstrates that mastery by performing the skill in front of the students. In this way, the students can learn by *imitation*. Jesus did this to perfection with His disciples, both teaching them and setting an example for them to imitate. This is also the prime quality of a godly leader. The godly leader does not say, "Go forth and do it," but, " Watch me, and do the same."

Prayer should precede action. Nehemiah was filled with anger when he learned his co-laborers had given their all for the Lord's work—sacrificing home, security, daily responsibilities, and even food—and been rewarded by being made paupers and sold into slavery. What's far worse, their own brethren had committed this crime! The nobles and rulers of the land were the very people who should have been setting an example of living by God's Word, but they were living more like the pagans around them for the sake of personal gain. If ever there was a time for righteous anger, this was it.

However, Nehemiah's first response was to give the matter some serious thought. He didn't need to think about whether their behavior was wrong, but he did need to think about what the Lord would have him do to correct that wrong. We can be confident, based on Nehemiah's responses to other crises, that he spent ample time on his knees before the Lord, perhaps even fasting before acting. He knew that if he responded in anger, he would be following the lead of his flesh—and he wanted to follow the lead of the Holy Spirit instead.

The psalmist wrote, "The LORD is gracious and full of compassion, slow to anger and great in mercy. The LORD is good to all, and His tender mercies are over all His works" (Psalm 145:8–9). Solomon gave us this practical advice: "A soft answer turns away wrath, but a harsh word stirs up anger. The tongue of the wise uses knowledge rightly, but the mouth of fools pours forth foolishness. . . . Better is a dinner of herbs where love is, than a fatted calf with hatred. A wrathful man stirs up strife, but he who is slow to anger allays contention" (Proverbs 15:1–2, 17–18). When anger arises—even righteous indignation—we must take time to seek the Lord in prayer and reflect on how He would have us respond.

REFLECTING ON THE TEXT

5) Why did Nehemiah give serious thought to the situation with the nobles and rulers before addressing them? In practical terms, how is this done? Why is it important?

_____

_____

_____

6) What were "the governor's provisions" (Nehemiah 5:14)? Why did Nehemiah not take advantage of what was his by right? How did this influence his rebuke of the nobles?

_____

_____

_____

7) How did Nehemiah demonstrate both courage and wisdom in repelling all of the enemies' strategies against him? What do you learn from his example?

---

8) When has someone taken advantage of your misfortunes? When have you been guilty of doing that to others? What did Jesus teach on this subject?

PERSONAL RESPONSE

9) When you find yourself in an emotionally charged situation, how do you usually respond? How does your normal response compare with Nehemiah's? How does it compare with Christ's response?

---

10) What leadership roles do you hold (parent, teacher, boss, group leader)? Do you tend to lead more by example or by command? Explain.

_____

_____

_____

_____

11

WORSHIPING GOD

Nehemiah 9:1–38

DRAWING NEAR

What are some of the ways today that people picture God? What qualities and attributes do they tend to assign to Him?

_____

_____

_____

THE CONTEXT

Now that the walls of Jerusalem were completed, the people of Judah could finally settle back into their homes. In celebration, the people gathered together less than a week after finishing the walls to observe the Feast of Tabernacles (see Leviticus 23:33–44). At the end of that feast, the people gathered once more to worship God as a reunited nation, humbling themselves and acknowledging their dependence on Him.

The Israelites had certainly endured many trials. They had been attacked by enemies from without and put into slavery by greedy nobles from within. Yet they had endured because of God's protection and provision for them. In the end, we find Ezra's public reading of the Word of God pricking the hearts of these weary wall-builders. They are reminded of God's greatness and their own failure to adequately live for His glory. Together, as a people, they confess their sins and worship the Lord their God.

This final study will require some self-examination on our part, which can certainly be a humbling and painful experience. Yet if we are to fully understand God's grace and mercy, we must also understand our own condition as sinners. And if we are to praise Him for His love and mercy, we must also remind ourselves of all He has done on our behalf. Just as the people of the newly reconstituted nation understood this truth, so must we as followers of Christ.

KEYS TO THE TEXT

Read Nehemiah 9:1–38, noting the key words and phrases indicated below.

THE PEOPLE PREPARE FOR WORSHIP: The Jews assemble in Jerusalem for a time of national worship and repentance. Before they begin, however, they prepare themselves.

1. ON THE TWENTY-FOURTH DAY OF THIS MONTH: This event took place in the Jewish month of Tishri, which would be September–October of 445 BC.

WITH FASTING, IN SACKCLOTH, AND WITH DUST ON THEIR HEADS: These were outward demonstrations on the people's part of deep mourning and sadness for their sins. Their actions seem to have been performed in the spirit of the Day of Atonement, which was observed on the tenth day of this same month.

2. SEPARATED THEMSELVES FROM ALL FOREIGNERS: It was necessary to again call the Jews to divorce all lawful wives taken from among the heathen because the previous call—prompted thirteen years before by Ezra—had been only partially successful. Many among the people had escaped the required action of divorce and kept their pagan wives. Perhaps new defaulters had now also appeared and were confronted for the first time with this necessary action of divorce. Nehemiah's efforts were successful in removing this evil mixture.

3. READ FROM THE BOOK OF THE LAW . . . CONFESSED AND WORSHIPED: God's Word is the foundation of the worship process. Its truths

confront the sin in our lives, and at the same time they reveal the character of God. Apart from God's Word there is no way to know Him, and so the rest of this prayer is built on the foundation of the study of the Word.

5. STAND UP AND BLESS THE LORD: The Levites led the people in a corporate outpouring of confession and worship. It was a time of national humility and public confession, set against the backdrop of God's great mercy and forgiveness. The end result of the three-hour worship service was a national promise of obedience to God in the future (see verse 38).

BEFORE THE BEGINNING: The Levites lead the people in worship chronologically through the history of Israel. They begin at the best place—before the beginning.

6. YOU ALONE ARE THE LORD: The worship service began with a fundamental truth: there is only one God, and He alone rules all things in heaven and on earth. It was important for the people to begin with this foundational understanding, for they had already been yielding to the temptation to embrace the beliefs of the world, which included a vast pantheon of make-believe gods. The Levites also were leading the people through a chronological remembrance of who God is and what He had done for them, so it was appropriate for them to begin before the world was even created, when God alone existed.

YOU HAVE MADE HEAVEN: This was a summary of God's creation, which encompasses not merely heaven and earth but also absolutely all that exists. God created everything, and He did so in six twenty-four-hour days. The Jews were reminding themselves that the world's teachings were utterly false concerning the origins of man.

7. WHO CHOSE ABRAM: It was the Lord God who had called Abraham, not Abraham who had sought out God. The Lord chose Abraham simply because He wanted to set His love on him, and He had been faithful ever since to the promises He had made (see Genesis 12; 17).

8. YOU FOUND HIS HEART FAITHFUL BEFORE YOU: Abraham had demonstrated a determination to obey the Lord's commands, as most clearly illustrated in his willingness to sacrifice his only son at God's request (see Genesis 22). Unfortunately, Abraham's descendants did not exhibit the same level of faithfulness to God's Word.

You have performed Your words: One of the themes of this song of praise is that God always keeps His promises, and He alone is righteous.

The Exodus: The prayer now moves forward in time to the period when the Israelites were slaves in Egypt and follows them on their exodus to the Promised Land.

10. signs and wonders against Pharaoh: The Lord had sent a series of ten plagues against the people of Egypt for their hardness of heart in refusing to allow His people to leave. The final plague was the death of every firstborn son in every household within Egypt, except those that were covered by the blood of a lamb on the doorposts. This event led to the annual celebration of Passover, and it also pictured the eventual sacrifice for sin offered by Christ on the cross.

11. You divided the sea before them: The Lord allowed His people to encounter an immovable obstacle—the Red Sea—while witnessing their enemies hard on their heels behind them. The Lord miraculously parted the sea before them, allowed them to walk across on dry ground, and slammed the sea shut on the heads of those same powerful enemies (see Exodus 14). God sometimes leads us through difficult circumstances in order to demonstrate His omnipotent sovereignty in our lives.

12. cloudy pillar . . . pillar of fire: The Lord made His presence known to the people of Israel night and day during their exodus from Egypt. During the day, He provided an immense cloud covering that shielded them from the hot desert sun. By night, He provided some sort of flaming element in the sky above, which allowed them to see in the utter darkness. These miraculous displays served the Israelites, but they also made known God's presence to the world around.

13. just ordinances and true laws: The Lord also came among His people during their journey and taught them how to live according to His plan. The Law that God gave to Moses was designed to make the Jews noticeably different from the rest of the world, so that other nations would see the goodness and uniqueness of Israel's God.

15. bread from heaven . . . water out of the rock: Both the manna from heaven (see Exodus 16) and the water from the rock (see Exodus 17) miraculously provided for the Israelites' physical needs in a dry and barren

land. But they also provided small pictures of God's ultimate plan of salvation through His Son Jesus, who is the "bread of life" (John 6:35).

> A MISERABLE CONTRAST: *The Levites now turn their attention from God's character to their own as they consider the ungodly behavior of their forefathers and themselves.*

16. THEY AND OUR FATHERS ACTED PROUDLY: The comparison between God's character and the character of the people did not paint a pretty picture. Interestingly, the Levites used the same phrase "acted proudly" to describe Pharaoh and the Egyptians (see verse 10), which implies that God's chosen people had proved to be no different from the world. They had hardened their necks just as Pharaoh had hardened his heart and stubbornly refused to obey God's commands.

17. THEY WERE NOT MINDFUL OF YOUR WONDERS: The Lord had performed countless dramatic miracles to demonstrate His power and presence, yet the people had ignored them. It was not even that they were not paying attention and didn't notice, but that they had deliberately refused to acknowledge God's faithfulness. They had made themselves blind by choice.

THEY APPOINTED A LEADER: The Hebrew of this statement is almost a repeat of Numbers 14:4, which records the dissatisfaction of the people with God's plan and Moses' leadership.

BUT YOU ARE GOD: Two of the most joyful words in Scripture are *but God*. The Israelites had deliberately hardened their hearts, but God had remained faithful. They had sinned in every way, but God had remained ready to pardon them. They had wandered away from Him repeatedly, but God had not forsaken them. The entire human race deserves God's wrath, but God provides the free gift of salvation.

18. THEY MADE A MOLDED CALF FOR THEMSELVES: The human heart is constantly seeking to make gods from the material world (see Exodus 32)— the world that was created by the only true God. This trend has not changed in modern times.

20. YOUR GOOD SPIRIT TO INSTRUCT THEM: Christians can say this with an even greater significance, as God sends His Holy Spirit to reside in the life of every believer (see John 14:26).

21. THEY LACKED NOTHING: Even during an extended time of discipline for stubborn sin, the Lord still met the people's every need. They wandered in the wilderness for forty years, but their clothes and shoes never wore out!

POSSESSION TO PRESENT: The Levites now move through the time when Israel took possession of the Promised Land and continue up to the present moment in Judah.

23. MULTIPLIED THEIR CHILDREN: Another aspect of the promise God made to Abraham was that he would be the father of a great nation (see Genesis 12:1–3). God told Abraham that his seed would be like the stars of heaven (see Genesis 15:5), and multiplication of the children of Israel in the land of Egypt had been nothing short of miraculous (see Exodus 1:1–3).

24. SUBDUED BEFORE THEM: Moses had once said, "The LORD is a man of war" (Exodus 15:3). As Israel's military leader and king, God had led them into battle to defeat their enemies and take the land.

26. NEVERTHELESS THEY WERE DISOBEDIENT: *But God* are two joyful words in Scripture, but the word *nevertheless* here is a sorrowful one. The Lord had poured out blessing after blessing on His people and demonstrated His power, sovereignty, faithfulness, and love. *Nevertheless*, the people remained rebellious and disobedient. Humankind is no different today.

WHO TESTIFIED AGAINST THEM: God's prophets had brought the people into God's court to be judged by His law. This theme is repeated throughout the prayer (see verses 29, 30, 34).

32. NOW THEREFORE: The Levites, having reviewed the faithfulness of God to the Abrahamic covenant throughout Israel's history, now turn to the present. They begin by confessing the people's unfaithfulness to God.

KINGS OF ASSYRIA . . . THIS DAY: This statement sweeps across a summary of Assyrian, Babylonian, and Persian domination of the nation for almost four centuries up to that time.

33. YOU ARE JUST IN ALL THAT HAS BEFALLEN US: The people asked the Lord to help them in their present distresses, yet they still recognized those distresses had befallen them because of their sin. They did not blame God, but they also did not refrain from asking for His mercy.

36. HERE WE ARE, SERVANTS IN IT: The Levites rejoiced that the Jews had been returned to the land, but grieved that Gentiles still ruled over them.

37. MUCH INCREASE TO THE KINGS: Because God's people continued in widespread sin, enemy kings enjoyed the bounty that would have belonged to Israel.

38. BECAUSE OF ALL THIS, WE MAKE A SURE COVENANT: The history of God's faithfulness, in spite of Israel's unfaithfulness, formed the ground of a pledge and promise the people made to obey God and not repeat the sins of their fathers. A covenant was a binding agreement between two parties—a formalized relationship with commitments to loyalty. In this case, the nation of Israel initiated this covenant with God.

UNLEASHING THE TEXT

1) What preparations did the people make before spending time in worship? What did these things mean? Why were they important? What parallels might they have in your life?

_____

_____

_____

_____

2) Why did the Levites work chronologically through the history of Israel in their worship? How might this help a person recognize both God's goodness and his or her sin?

_____

_____

_____

_____

3) Why did the worship begin with God's preexistence and role as creator of the universe? In what sense are these truths fundamental to an accurate understanding of His character?

_____

_____

_____

_____

4) What miraculous provisions did God make for His people throughout Israel's history? What miraculous provisions has He made in your life?

_____

_____

_____

EXPLORING THE MEANING

God is the creator and sustainer of the universe. Before anything existed, God was present. He is beyond and apart from everything, self-sustaining and self-sufficient. Even His name "I AM" suggests this (Exodus 3:14). God created all things that exist in just six days, and created everything with the mere power of His Word: "God said . . . and there was" (Genesis 1:3). He called the stars into existence and fixed them in place, created the sun and moon to give light to the earth, and created the earth and the heavens to manifest the glory of His character.

But God did not create the universe and then walk away to do something else. He continues to maintain His creation and demonstrate His love for everything He made—especially people. This is what the Levites had in mind when they said to God, "You preserve them all" (Nehemiah 9:6). God preserves and sustains His entire creation. He controls all events in a constant unfolding of His perfect plan through His absolute sovereignty—a plan that He had in mind before the beginning, before the creation of the universe.

God is both eternal and immutable. He has always existed, with no beginning and no ending, yet He has not changed in any way since before creation. He is the same yesterday, today, and forever (see Hebrews 13:8). His plan to bring salvation to all people has been unfolding since before the beginning of time, and His plan to complete His work of salvation will continue through the end of the ages. This is one of the many reasons we join the Levites in finding God worthy of worship and praise!

God is gracious, even with the presumptuous. The constant theme of the Levites' praise was the graciousness of God. In fact, the entire prayer is a litany of God's acts of compassion toward His people. Ever since the first sin plunged all of humanity into sin, God has been graciously working to bring peace and reconciliation to the earth. After Adam sinned, God told the serpent that from Eve's "seed" would come a Man who would crush Satan (see Genesis 3:15). From that point forward, history—much of which was recounted by the Levites in this chapter—has been leading up to that Person.

In the meantime, the world continued to rebel, and God continued to respond to each rebellion with a mixture of punishment, discipline, and graciousness. He destroyed the world, yet started over with one family. He scattered the nations when He shattered the Tower of Babel, but He then chose one new nation from whom He would bless all the families of the earth. When that new nation, Israel, rebelled against Him in the wilderness, God disciplined them but also guided them through their wanderings by way of a cloud and supernatural light.

God was faithful and gracious to His people during Moses' day, and He is still faithful and gracious to His people today. The difference is that now God has sent His Son in the ultimate act of His graciousness. Jesus came as a sacrifice for sin, and in the consummate act of kindness, He gave His life for people who hated Him and wanted Him dead. As a result, the news of the gospel is really the news that God's graciousness has conquered the hearts of presumptuous sinners. Jesus' grace is stronger than the hardest of sinners' hearts.

Praise God for His attributes. Meditate on some of God's attributes below, and then spend time in prayer thanking God for who He is.

Omniscience: God knows all things, and there is nothing hidden from Him (see Revelation 2:23).

Alpha and Omega, Beginning and End: God described Himself as "I AM WHO I AM" (Exodus 3:14; Revelation 1:8). He sustains all things in the universe that He created, and without Him nothing could exist.

Ready to pardon: Jesus demonstrated this quality at the very point of His death, calling on the Father to forgive the ones who crucified Him (see Luke 23:34).

Gracious and merciful: God pours out mercy and tenderness on His creation, even when we deserve His judgment (see Hebrews 2:17).

Slow to anger: Throughout the ages, God's people have frequently put His grace to the test and persisted in stubborn sin despite His goodness— yet He has held back His hand of judgment (see Psalm 103:8).

Keeps covenant and mercy: The Levites recognized this attribute of God's character as they worked their way through the history of Israel. The Lord's people frequently violated their covenant with God, but God never failed to keep it and to show mercy on them (see Nehemiah 9:32).

REFLECTING ON THE TEXT

5) In what ways did Israel betray God throughout its history? Why did God continually forgive and restore the people? What does this reveal about God?

_____

_____

_____

_____

6) Consider God's triune nature: Father, Son, and Holy Spirit. How is each person unique? How are all three perfectly united? How might these truths influence your worship?

_____

_____

_____

_____

7) Why is worship important to individual Christians? Why is it important to the church as a whole? What is involved in worshiping the Lord?

_____

_____

_____

_____

8) What are some other attributes of God's nature that you could add to the above list?

_____

_____

_____

_____

PERSONAL RESPONSE

9) What are some shortcomings and failures that you are willing to confess in your life? Spend some time in self-reflection to acknowledge your sins and repent of them.

_____

_____

_____

10) How do you see God's graciousness triumphing over sin in your own life?

_____

_____

_____

12

REVIEWING KEY PRINCIPLES

DRAWING NEAR

As you look back at each of the studies, what is the one thing that stood out to you the most? What is one new perspective you have learned?

_____

_____

_____

THE CONTEXT

During the course of these studies, we have watched as God's people made their way on the arduous move from Persia to Jerusalem, and we have considered the sacrifices they made to rebuild temple and the city walls. Indeed, many of the Jewish exiles had grown comfortable and prosperous in Persia and chose not to make the move back to Judah simply because the cost was too high. But there were others—like Ezra, Nehemiah, Haggai, and Zechariah—who did not hesitate to pay whatever cost was required to obey God's commands.

And hardship there was. God's people faced strong opposition from powerful enemies and endured mockery, sabotage, false friendship, and even death threats. Beyond that, the godly leaders came to realize that apart from the new covenant and the Messiah, the people would never be able to obey the Lord's commands. Yet through it all, God's character shines out. We are reminded at every turn that He is completely sovereign over all affairs of mankind, and we see again and again that He is faithful and true to His Word.

Here are a few of the major principles we have found during our study. There are many more we don't have room to reiterate, so take some time to review the earlier studies—or, better still, to meditate on the Scripture that we have covered. As you do, ask the Holy Spirit to give you wisdom and insight into His Word. He will not refuse.

Exploring the Meaning

This world is not our home. The people of Judah had been carried away to captivity, but they had not been made slaves as they were many centuries before in Egypt. Instead, they were allowed to establish relatively normal lives within the new land, and many of the Jews had risen to levels of power and prosperity. Daniel, for example, served at least three different kings as a close personal counselor. Yet this relative freedom brought a danger the Israelites had not faced when they were slaves: *complacency.* Many of God's people had become quite comfortable in captivity and were fitting in to the society and doing well.

The problem was that God did not intend for His people to make their permanent home outside of Judah. Their real home was there, and the Lord did not want them to put down roots anywhere else. God's temple in Jerusalem was in ruins, the city's walls lay in rubble, and the Lord grieved over that situation. He wanted His people to share His priorities and to long to return to their proper land where they would worship and serve Him as He had ordained. The world in which they had grown so content was *not* their home.

This is equally true for Christians today. This world is not our home! It is not wrong to pursue a career or to establish a home, but the Lord does not want us to lose our eternal focus. He wants us to remember that the things of eternity are what matter most, not the things of this world. Paul wrote, "Set your mind on things above, not on things on the earth. For you died, and your life is hidden with Christ in God" (Colossians 3:2–3). Paul was reminding us that by being born again into the salvation of Christ, we have died to the things of this world. And if we are dead to this world, there is no purpose in trying to make our home here. Our existence is with Christ in eternity, and that is where our focus needs to remain.

God commands us to resist discouragement. The enemies of God's people attempted to interrupt their works of obedience by causing them to become discouraged. The *King James Version* renders Ezra 4:4: "The people of the land weakened the hands of the people of Judah," which captures the essence of discouragement—to become weak, to sink down, to lose the ability to carry on, and to let God's projects drop from despair.

Fear is at the root of discouragement. We are suddenly faced with a circumstance that is beyond our control, and we quickly begin to fear that it is beyond *God's* control as well. And if it is beyond God's control, we might as well just give up now—which is, of course, precisely what Satan is hoping that we will do! However, God commands us to not give in to fear but to strengthen our hands when they become weak (see Isaiah 41:10; Hebrews 12:12).

The best way for us to do this, wrote the author of Hebrews, is to "consider Him who endured such hostility from sinners against Himself, lest you become weary and discouraged in your souls" (12:3). We must remember that Jesus Himself faced immense opposition—more severe than any we will ever face. Yet He overcame it all through the faithfulness of God and through utter confidence in and reliance on God's sovereignty.

It is wise to consider your ways. The Lord sent His prophet Haggai to bring one clear message to His people: obey God even when the circumstances are difficult. The prophet proclaimed, "Consider your ways!" (Haggai 1:5). This command might be translated, "Set your mind on your way of life." In other words, it was a call for the people to consider their ultimate priorities. In effect, God proclaimed, "Make *your* priorities *My* priorities!"

This is an important discipline that God's people need to exercise on a regular basis. The priorities and perspectives of the world are *not* God's views, yet they have a way of seeping into our thinking without our even being aware of it. As Christians, we need to reassess our priorities and views daily, even moment by moment, to ensure that we are thinking the way God thinks. We do this by spending time daily studying and meditating on His Word, by seeking His wisdom through prayer, and by fellowshipping with other believers.

Paul warns his readers that this process is vital if we are to understand God's will for our lives. "I beseech you therefore, brethren, by the mercies of God, that you present your bodies a living sacrifice, holy, acceptable to God, which is your reasonable service. And do not be conformed to this world, but be transformed by the renewing of your mind, that you may prove what is that good and acceptable and perfect will of God" (Romans 12:1–2). Christians cannot hope to understand God's perfect will unless they are constantly renewing their minds by the Word of God. If we forget to consider our ways, we will wind up conformed to this world.

The Lord yearns for our fellowship. The Lord told His people, "I am zealous for Zion with great zeal; with great fervor I am zealous for her" (Zechariah 8:2). Many modern Bibles translate "fervor" as "wrath," which captures the burning passion the Lord was expressing. "I burn for you with a jealous fire," the Lord was effectively saying, "a zealous and jealous love that will tolerate no competition." The Lord yearned so deeply for the fellowship of His people that it was like a consuming fire, destroying anything that prevented their full reconciliation.

It is interesting that the Lord referred to the zeal of His love in this context. The Jews had been zealous themselves in maintaining a cycle of fasts over a period of seventy years during their captivity. "Should I weep in the fifth month and fast as I have done for so many years?" they asked (Zechariah 7:3). Their question implied that they had not permitted anything to prevent them from keeping this religious observance, but the Lord called them to search their hearts and question why they were truly fasting. Were they mourning the loss of God's close fellowship, which they had once enjoyed as His chosen nation? Or were they mourning over their own suffering and misfortune? The two were not the same!

The Lord wanted His people to be zealous in seeking His face and entering His holy presence. Now, this might well be associated with certain spiritual activities, such as commemorating the Lord's Supper as Jesus commanded (see Luke 22), but those activities themselves are hollow and meaningless if one's heart is not fully committed to living in fellowship with God. The Lord has a burning zeal for our fellowship, for our company, and He wants us to have that same zeal for Him.

There are no shortcuts in obedience to God's Word. Ezra made many preparations for the move to Jerusalem. He gathered a large body of Jews to join him, and each of those families made all the necessary preparations involved in making a life-changing move. The king had given Ezra his full blessing on the trip and provided him with a letter of authority to reestablish a Jewish community and rebuild the Lord's temple. The king had also handed Ezra a huge sum of money and treasure, and Ezra probably felt a sense of urgency to get that money where it belonged. A host of people and plans were ready to go. But then Ezra made the startling discovery that there were no members of the tribe of Levi with him on the journey.

Human wisdom would suggest a "work-around" measure at this point. So many people were standing around, waiting to get started, and the king's money was just sitting there waiting for theft. Surely, under such circumstances, prudence would dictate an "ad hoc" alternate plan. But Ezra refused to begin rebuilding the temple without the leadership and assistance of God's selected priests because God's Word commanded it. Ezra may have been caught by surprise, but he knew that the Lord was not. God wanted him to follow His prescribed methods, and He would take care of the timetable.

There are no shortcuts to obeying God's Word. The Lord does not call His people to find "work-arounds" or "emergency interim methods." His Word gives clear guidance in our daily lives, the correct approach to worship and church structure, roles of authority and submission, and much more that often goes contrary to what the world believes today. When it comes to the clear teachings in Scripture, there is no substitute for obedience.

Service is crucial, especially when it's costly. Nehemiah lived in Persia, the greatest and wealthiest nation of its day. Furthermore, he lived in Susa, the nation's capital and one of the richest and most comfortable of the Persian cities. To top this off, he was the cupbearer to the king himself, a position of high trust and influence. He was undoubtedly rich and high in the ranks of the most powerful nation on earth. Jerusalem was far away—a journey of three full months. It would have been easy for Nehemiah to forget about his people.

Yet when he heard about the plight of his fellow Jews in far-off Judah, he mourned, wept, fasted, and prayed. What's more, he determined in his heart to forsake all the blessings and comforts of Persia and exchange them for hard work, rough living conditions, and constant hatred and opposition from God's enemies. In fact, Nehemiah was so determined to help with the work in Jerusalem that he risked his own life to get there. He put himself in peril of the king's wrath by making the request to leave the king's service, and then he embarked on the dangerous and uncomfortable trip to Judah.

It was not wrong or sinful for Nehemiah to enjoy the comforts of Persia and the king's court. The Lord had placed him in this position, and Nehemiah was being faithful to the tasks God had given him. But the Lord had placed him there specifically so that he might be positioned to help the Jews at this moment of crisis, just as He had placed Esther where she could save the Jews from annihilation a generation earlier (see Esther 4:14). The Lord was calling Nehemiah to voluntarily forsake all these blessings to participate in an important project, and the blessings that came from his obedience far surpassed all the comforts of the king's palace. When the Lord calls us in a similar way, we must always heed the call, for our obedience will bring glory to His name and great blessings to us.

We must be alert and prepared for battle. Nehemiah didn't take the enemy's threat lightly when he learned they were planning to slaughter the Jews. He knew, of course, that the true protection of God's people lay solely in God's hands, but he also understood that he had a responsibility for the safety and welfare of those under his authority. Consequently, he took strong steps to prepare for the threat of battle. What's more, he expected all those working on the Lord's project to also remain alert and well armed. It must have been a real hindrance to the work of building, which was strenuous enough without having only one hand available, but Nehemiah felt the work of self-defense was as important as the work of rebuilding the wall.

Most of us do not face the threat of physical violence for our faith (though there are many Christians in parts of the world who do), but this principle applies at least as much on the spiritual level. Even if our neighbors are not threatening to attack us, we all face an enemy who is deadlier than those who opposed the Jews. For this reason, God commands us through His Word to be constantly on guard against the forces of wickedness, and He also commands us to go everywhere well armed. As Paul instructs, we are to carry with us "the sword of the Spirit, which is the word of God" (Ephesians 6:17). The writer of Hebrews gives this further detail: "For the word of God is living and powerful, and sharper than any two-edged sword, piercing even to the division of soul and spirit, and of joints and marrow, and is a discerner of the thoughts and intents of the heart" (Hebrews 4:12).

Well-armed and vigilant Christians spend time reading and meditating daily on the Word of God. And like all well-trained soldiers, believers in Christ also stay in close contact with the Commanding Officer through prayer and obedience. The military analogy, in fact, is apt in life, because we live in a battle zone where the enemy is constantly trying to destroy us. Therefore, we must always "be sober, be vigilant; because your adversary the devil walks about like a roaring lion, seeking whom he may devour. Resist him, steadfast in the faith, knowing that the same sufferings are experienced by your brotherhood in the world" (1 Peter 5:8–9).

God is the creator and sustainer of the universe. Before anything existed, God was present. He is beyond and apart from everything, self-sustaining and self-sufficient. Even His name "I Am" suggests this (Exodus 3:14). God created all things that exist in just six days, and created everything with the mere power of His Word: "God said . . . and there was" (Genesis 1:3). He called the stars into existence and fixed them in place, created the sun and moon to give light to the earth, and created the earth and the heavens to manifest the glory of His character.

But God did not create the universe and then walk away to do something else. He continues to maintain His creation and demonstrate His love for everything He made—especially people. This is what the Levites had in mind when they said to God, "You preserve them all" (Nehemiah 9:6). God preserves and sustains His entire creation. He controls all events in a constant unfolding of His perfect plan through His absolute sovereignty—a plan that He had in mind before the beginning, before the creation of the universe.

God is both eternal and immutable. He has always existed, with no beginning and no ending, yet He has not changed in any way since before creation. He is the same yesterday, today, and forever (see Hebrews 13:8). His plan to bring salvation to all people has been unfolding since before the beginning of time, and His plan to complete His work of salvation will continue through the end of the ages. This is one of the many reasons we join the Levites in finding God worthy of worship and praise!

UNLEASHING THE TEXT

1) Which of the concepts or principles in this study have you found to be the most encouraging? Why?

_____

_____

_____

2) Which of the concepts or principles have you found most challenging? Why?

_____

_____

_____

3) What aspects of "walking with God" are you already doing in your life? Which areas need strengthening?

_____

_____

_____

4) To which of the characters that we've studied have you most been able to relate? How might you emulate that person in your own life?

_____

_____

_____

PERSONAL RESPONSE

5) Have you taken a definite stand for Jesus Christ? Have you accepted His free gift of salvation? If not, what is preventing you from doing so?

_____

_____

_____

6) What areas of your life have been most convicted during this study? What exact things will you do to address these convictions? Be specific.

_____

_____

_____

7) What have you learned about the character of God during this study? How has this insight affected your worship or prayer life?

_____

_____

_____

8) What are some specific things you want to see God do in your life in the coming month? What are some things you intend to change in your own life during that time? (Return to this list in one month and hold yourself accountable to fulfill these things.)

_____

_____

_____

If this is the first of these studies that you have completed, read the previous titles in this series. They will greatly enhance your knowledge of the Old Testament—not to mention your walk with God.

ALSO AVAILABLE

I n this study, John MacArthur guides readers through an
in-depth look at the historical period beginning with
God's calling of Moses, continuing through the giving of the
Ten Commandments, and concluding with the Israelites'
preparations to enter the Promised Land. This study includes
close-up examinations of Aaron, Caleb, Joshua, Balaam and
Balak, as well as careful considerations of doctrinal themes such
as "Complaints and Rebellion" and "Following God's Law."

The MacArthur Bible Studies provide intriguing examinations of the whole of Scripture. Each guide incorporates
extensive commentary, detailed observations on overriding
themes, and probing questions to help you study the Word of
God with guidance from John MacArthur.

ALSO AVAILABLE

In this study, John MacArthur guides readers through an in-depth look at the Israelites' conquest of the Promised Land, beginning with the miraculous parting of the Jordan River, continuing through the victories and setbacks as the people settled into Canaan, and concluding with the time of the judges. Studies include close-up examinations of Rahab, Ruth, and Samson, as well as careful considerations of doctrinal themes such as "The Sin of Achan" and the role of "The Kinsman Redeemer."

The MacArthur Bible Studies provide intriguing examinations of the whole of Scripture. Each guide incorporates extensive commentary, detailed observations on overriding themes, and probing questions to help you study the Word of God with guidance from John MacArthur.

ALSO AVAILABLE

In this study, John MacArthur guides readers through an in-depth look at this historical period beginning with the miraculous birth of Samuel, continuing through Saul's crowning as Israel's first king, and concluding with his tragic death. Studies include close-up examinations of Hannah, Eli, Saul, David, and Jonathan, as well as careful considerations of doctrinal themes such as "Slaying a Giant" and "Respecting God's Anointed."

The MacArthur Bible Studies provide intriguing examinations of the whole of Scripture. Each guide incorporates extensive commentary, detailed observations on overriding themes, and probing questions to help you study the Word of God with guidance from John MacArthur.

ALSO AVAILABLE

In this study, John MacArthur guides readers through an in-depth look at the historical period beginning with David's struggle to establish his throne, continuing through his sin and repentance, and concluding with the tragic rebellion of his son Absalom. Studies include close-up examinations of Joab, Amnon, Tamar, Absalom, and others, as well as careful considerations of doctrinal themes such as "Obedience and Blessing" and being a "Man After God's Own Heart."

The MacArthur Bible Studies provide intriguing examinations of the whole of Scripture. Each guide incorporates extensive commentary, detailed observations on overriding themes, and probing questions to help you study the Word of God with guidance from John MacArthur.